DATE DUE

JAN 0 2 2002			

Demco, Inc. 38-293

DAVID A. WAITE
WILLIAM T. HEARTZ
W. DAVID McCORMACK

Integrated Performance Assurance

*How to Combine
Your Quality,
Environmental,
and Health & Safety
Management
Systems*

QUALITY RESOURCES.

A Division of The Kraus Organization Limited
New York, New York

Most Quality Resources books are available at quantity discounts when purchased in bulk. For more information contact:

Special Sales Department
Quality Resources
A Division of the Kraus Organization Limited
902 Broadway   800-247-8519
New York, New York 10010   212-979-8600
www.qualityresources.com   E-mail: info@qualityresources.com

Printed in the United States of America

02 01 00 99 98   10 9 8 7 6 5 4 3 2 1
                    ∞
The paper used in this publication meets the minimum requirements of American National Standard for Information Sciences—Permanence of Paper for Printed Library Materials, ANSI Z39.48-1984.

ISBN 0-527-76342-X

Library of Congress Cataloging-in-Publication Data

Waite, D. A.
        Integrated performance assurance : how to combine your quality, environmental, and health and safety management systems / David A. Waite, William T. Heartz, David McCormack.
          p.   cm.
        Includes bibliographical references and index..
        ISBN 0-527-76342-X (alk. paper)
        1. Industrial management—Cost effectiveness. 2. Organizational effectiveness. 3. Quality assurance—Management. 4. Industrial safety—Management. I. Heartz, William T. II. McCormack, David (W. David) III. Title.
HD31.W244   1997
658—dc21   97-41248
                                                        CIP

        HD 31 .W244 1998

        Waite, D. A.

        Integrated performance
          assurance : how to

TABLE OF CONTENTS

LIST OF EXHIBITS

PREFACE

This book presents a framework for answering the following questions: "Should I integrate my performance assurance programs?" and "Will it be cost-effective for my company?" It then provides practical approaches and suggestions for planning and implementing an integrated performance assurance (IPA) program and incorporating that program into your company's existing business and operations management processes.

This book has a number of potential audiences. One is the company executive or line manager seeking to move the company forward as a truly effective business enterprise. This book describes an approach for integrating and streamlining the processes to ensure the company meets *all* of its business objectives in a consistent, systematic, and client-focused manner. Readers may have specific issues or concerns related to worker health and safety, compliance with environmental regulations, pollution prevention, or the quality of company products and services.

Another audience is managers of performance assurance, human health and safety, quality assurance, environmental compliance or protection, or other organizations. These managers seek ways to reenergize and refocus their companies on performance issues and processes. This book offers an integrated approach that brings the multiple areas of performance assurance together and infuses them into the companies' business and operational processes, and a flexible approach that can be tailored to focus evenly on all performance areas, or adjusted to emphasize specific issues or performance areas, if appropriate. Regardless of focus, all performance programs and operations are enhanced.

Quality managers will find approaches to integrate quality processes within their companies' performance assurance functions as well as throughout business and operations management systems. Safety managers will find approaches to achieve behavior-based safety by adopting it as a core business value and aligning that core value with the companies' management systems. Compliance managers will find approaches for achieving systematic compliance assurance during operational activities by adopting company core values and management system alignment.

Sean Hawley added a great deal to this book by conducting research on the application of the IPA approach to organizations worldwide as well as providing a business and financial perspective. We gratefully acknowledge the case examples supplied by Dr. Andrea Oliva of the Sistemí Gestionalì Ecocompatibíli, Oderzo, Italy. Our employer, CH2M Hill, is also due thanks for encouraging production of the book by providing funding and some of the case histories.

INTRODUCTION

In today's intensely competitive marketplace, companies concerned about financial performance, growth, and shareholder value cannot ignore their business risks, which include failure to comply with the many regulations applicable to a given business endeavor. This may be a lack of environmental protection, failure to adequately protect the safety and health of workers and (in certain cases) clients or customers, and failure to meet the customer's requirements, product expectations, and service quality. In today's regulated and litigious environment (where a single failure to manage critical risks can lead to complete failure of a business), it has become particularly important that companies adopt management processes to manage risks systematically over the full life cycle of their activities. Effective risk management and loss-prevention programs also provide direct savings in business insurance costs and increased bonding capacity in service industries.

Businesses now realize that excellence in compliance, environmental safety and health protection, and quality assurance performance is good business and can contribute to financial success. Clients increasingly demand such performance from their suppliers. In the United States, for example, the federal government, through its procurement-streamlining legislation, requires that performance histories be included in federal procurement decisions. In private industry, contractor selections are now based on safety records, and incentive fee programs are beginning to include both quality and safety criteria. Further, with the development of national and international management system standards, performance in these areas is becoming a de facto criterion for participation in the global marketplace.

The challenge facing businesses in their implementation of risk management and performance assurance systems is to maximize their value added, while minimizing their cost. These programs must be both cost-effective and reliable; integrated performance assurance (IPA) provides a mechanism to improve cost-effectiveness and reliability by taking advantage of the synergy among risk mitigation disciplines.

WHAT IS INTEGRATED PERFORMANCE ASSURANCE?

Industry has traditionally managed its compliance, environmental safety and health protection, and quality assurance functions as separate programs because they originate at separate points in time, are driven by distinct regulatory agency and customer criteria, and employ separate technical disciplines. A traditional stove-pipe approach was reasonable and probably unavoidable when these systems were first introduced. However, various influences have combined to produce conditions that now make an integrated approach to the management and execution of these systems desirable. These influences are summarized here and discussed in detail in chapter 1, "Why Integrate?"

Examination of compliance, environmental safety and health protection, and quality assurance programs reveals many similarities:

- They serve common underlying objectives (i.e., performance assurance or risk management).

- They use common approaches to achieve those objectives (i.e., activity-specific evaluation, planning, and oversight).

- They share common success and failure measures (i.e., cost, schedule, violations, and liabilities).

Integrating economical management of these programs is advantageous because of the growing emphasis on high-quality environmental compliance (and recently health and safety) system standards. Primarily criteria-based regulations are now being supplemented by management system standards. The emerging regulatory model has an integrated structure that embodies environmental safety and health protection, combined with quality and compliance standards and practices.

The importance of risk management to long-term business success—as well as recognition of the role that regulatory compliance, environmental protection, health and safety, and quality assurance programs play in managing critical risks—makes it desirable to integrate these programs with other core business management processes. For the sake of clarity, quality assurance (QA), as used in this book, is defined as follows: The integrated system of management processes involving planning, implementation, assessment, reporting, and quality improvement used collectively to assure that a project or service will be of the type and quality specified in the agreement with the client. Quality control (QC) is defined as the overall system of technical activities that measure the attributes and performance of a process, item, or service against defined standards to verify that they have met the established specifications of the project.

In its simplest terms, IPA assigns responsibility for management and execution of compliance, environmental safety and health protection, and quality assurance functions to a single, top-level organization. It employs a consolidated information system for identifying and responding to specific project activities and for tracking performance in each of the three areas. Within the IPA organization, individuals responsible for these areas coordinate development and execution of performance assurance plans based on shared performance criteria, goals, and priorities. Integrated measurement systems and feedback processes ensure that the desired level of performance is achieved and that performance improvement opportunities are realized.

As a key business management process, the IPA function, coupled with legal review, enables systematically achieving risk management objectives over an activity's full life cycle. Involving IPA staff at the initial goal-setting stage of an activity ensures that performance objectives are identified and included in the planning process. Explicit performance tasking is accomplished while developing written operating procedures where "we say what to do." Through effective training and communication, employee ownership is achieved, and "we do what we said" and "record what we did."

WHAT YOU WILL FIND IN THIS BOOK

STRUCTURE

This book is a hands-on, practical guide to implementing IPA. The authors provide step-by-step guidance applicable to a wide range of organizations. This process helps the reader evaluate whether IPA will benefit an organization; this is followed by a road map to implement and maintain an effective IPA management system. Tools include presentation slides and checklists to help the reader sell the concept and train staff during its implementation. This book is not intended as an academic reference, but as a how-to manual written in plain language and designed to help the reader move quickly from conception to final implementation in an organization.

CASE STUDIES

Throughout the book, case studies are provided by our employer, CH2M Hill, and some of its clients. CH2M Hill provides planning, engineering design, and operations and construction management services to help clients apply technology, safeguard the environment, and develop infrastructure.

ONE

WHY INTEGRATE?

INTRODUCTION

This chapter helps the reader answer the question, "Why Integrate?" or "Is IPA good business?" Providing a satisfactory answer may be as simple as answering the question, "Do you want to manage your risks while responding to clients' needs?" Assuming that the answer is not that simple, however, this chapter examines the expected characteristics of the most successful businesses of the next century. Next, the authors compare these characteristics with the offerings of the IPA approach to risk management by using a case study involving a specific set of client expectations.

ORGANIZATIONAL TRENDS

Go to almost any good library or bookstore and you will find shelf after shelf of books on present and future trends in business management practices. One of the most intriguing is

1

titled, *The Organization of the Future*, edited by Frances Hesselbein under the auspices of the Drucker Foundation. This book is a collection of articles on all aspects of future organizational characteristics. Although each of the 46 authors takes a slightly different approach to anticipating the future, several very strong individual themes emerge. The unifying theme is that, no matter how large an enterprise might be, it must interact with the customer and implement its policies and decisions as if it were a small business. The remainder of this section examines this concept.

Because of the greater relative importance of each individual customer to a small business, small businesses often stay closer to their customers and are more client-driven than larger businesses. Staying close pays great dividends if the small business operates in a flexible, agile mode, able to respond quickly to clients in a cost-competitive way. Being flexible reduces decision time and noticeably increases the ability of the business to respond to the specific needs of the customer, even to the extent of continually forming and reforming high-performance teams. This characteristic requires the absence of non-value-added functions, organizational boundaries, and artificial barriers to effective and efficient operation. It also enables a close partnership with the customer.

Another characteristic of a small business that is often lost in a larger organization is a high level of integration, without a corresponding high level of bureaucracy. Each member of the team must be an enabler for the other team members. Of course, this is driven by the need for everyone in a small organization to contribute in any way necessary to produce results and to further the overall goals of the organization. This mode of operation makes employee familiarity with and buy-in to the organizational mission and values very important. The mission keeps energies focused on value-added activities, while values communicate a culture that helps ensure day-to-day behaviors consistent with the organizational mission. This produces a cohesive group of activity sets, often in contrast to the historical command and control approach.

Therefore, the key characteristics of the successful business enterprise of the next century appear to be as follows:

- Stays close to the customer and is client-driven.

- Operates in a flexible, agile mode, able to respond quickly to client needs.

- Continuously forms and reforms high-performance teams as needed.

- Operates a highly integrated organization, without organizational boundaries and artificial barriers.

- Remains results-oriented.

- Obtains employee buy-in to mission and values.

We can now explore how the IPA approach fosters such characteristics in the context of a real set of customer expectations.

CASE STUDY

One of the clearest sets of client expectations ever communicated was issued in the 1980s, first by the U.S. Department of Energy (DOE), then by the U.S. Environmental Protection Agency (EPA), relative to environmental remediation at contaminated sites. The extensive publicity both agencies received concerning inefficiencies in their respective cleanup efforts drove development of this set of expectations. Data showed that the DOE's costs to clean up sites were much more than the private-sector rate. For the EPA, data showed that little Superfund financing was going to the actual site cleanup effort. This common motivation gave rise to "better," "cheaper," "faster," and "safer" as proposal evaluation criteria. All evaluations of potential offers would be based on these four criteria. In addition, it was understood that the data behind the remediation decisions and the cleanup work would have to continue to be of litigation quality. Clearly, the message was that business as usual was no longer acceptable to the DOE and the EPA.

CH2M HILL'S RESPONSE

Because the EPA was one of CH2M Hill's biggest customers, these new evaluation criteria required an immediate response. The company began by:

- Refining the project delivery process.

- Implementing the observational approach.

- Applying an IPA approach to risk management.

As data came to light for both the DOE and EPA cleanup efforts, it became apparent that many inefficiencies existed in the way cleanup projects were delivered on the contaminated sites. Some were easily recognizable, but others were lost in details of project delivery methods which, in general, were not well documented and were not often, if ever, closely analyzed for effectiveness and efficiency. To fully understand and document its project delivery process, CH2M Hill developed and refined the details of its process and published the results as *Project Delivery: A System and Process for Benchmark Performance.* As business environments became increasingly competitive, clients began to seek more comprehensive solutions to the delivery of their projects, and to maintain a competitive edge, CH2M Hill had to adapt to its clients' changing demands. The challenge was to develop a holistic approach aimed not only at technical solutions, but also at all aspects of project delivery. To meet this challenge, a process-driven project delivery system that incorporated the best principles and practices from total quality management, process improvement, and the organization's reengineering movement was developed.

Such a system offers benefits to clients, the firm, project managers, and project team members. For clients, the system leads to benchmark project performance and development of high-quality products. Improvements in client service occur as we consistently and routinely apply all components of the system. For the firm, the system provides a consistent client focus adaptable to the changing demands and challenges of the business environment and leads to increased firm profitability and growth. The system ensures that past problem areas are carefully managed and that any new problems are quickly identified and addressed. This type of system enables project managers to provide services and products with the greatest benefit to their clients. Through the system, they can incrementally build their skills as they address their clients' day-to-day needs. For project team members, the system provides a broad understanding of how and where they can make a difference in the successful delivery of products and services.

At the core of the project delivery system is client-focused application of those principles that most influence the performance of projects (depicted in Exhibit 1-1). These principles include the following:

- The project manager as leader.

- Client satisfaction.

- Consistent project planning and execution.

The DOE and EPA data also revealed that far too much money was being spent studying the sites, relative to actually cleaning them up. Many aspects of these study efforts were responses to the litigious nature of the work, a natural approach to risk management. However, it was clear that successful DOE and EPA contractors would have to demonstrate marked improvement in management of both risk and uncertainty. In response to this need, CH2M Hill adapted an approach to the remedial investigation portion of the Comprehensive Environmental Response, Compensation, and Liability Act of 1980 (CERCLA) process, called the observational approach.

Karl Terzaghi (Brown et al., 1989), a soil mechanics engineer, first developed systematic procedures for engineering under conditions of uncertainty. He called these procedures the "observational, experimental, or learn-as-you-go" method. He observed that vast amounts of effort are expended in much engineering work to secure only rough approximations of parameter values that appear in design calculations. Therefore, the

EXHIBIT 1–1. PROJECT DELIVERY SYSTEM COMPONENTS

results of these extensive calculations were little more than working hypotheses, subject to subsequent confirmation or modification.

In the past, only two methods were used for coping with the inevitable uncertainties: either adopt an excessive factor of safety or make assumptions consistent with general average experience. The first method is wasteful; the second is dangerous. A third method is depicted in Exhibit 1-2. The procedure is as follows: Base the engineering on whatever information can be secured. Make a detailed inventory of all the possible differences between reality and the assumptions. Then compute, on the basis of the original assumptions, various quantities that can be measured in the field. On the basis of such measurements, gradually close the gaps in knowledge and modify the engineering, if necessary.

Peck (1969) summarized the key elements in the practice of the observational method:

EXHIBIT 1–2. OBSERVATIONAL APPROACH

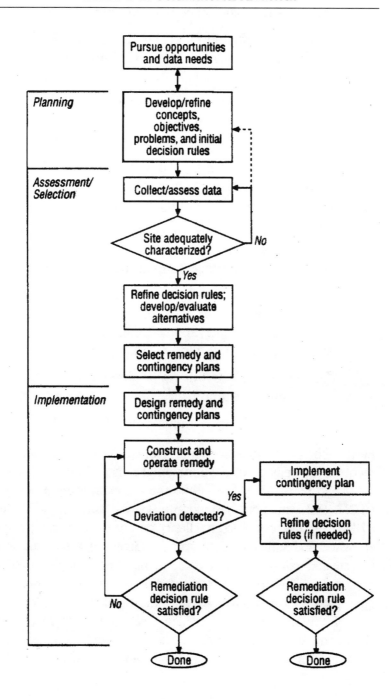

- Exploration sufficient to establish at least the general nature, pattern, and properties, but not in detail.

- Assessment of the most probable conditions and the most unfavorable conceivable deviations from these conditions.

- Establishment of the engineering based on the working hypothesis of the behavior that can be anticipated under the most probable conditions.

- Selection of quantities to be observed as the work proceeds and calculation of their anticipated values on the basis of the working hypothesis.

- Calculation of the same values of the same quantities under the most unfavorable conditions compatible with the available data concerning the actual conditions.

- Selection in advance of a course of action or modification of engineering for every foreseeable significant deviation of the observational findings from those predicted on the basis of the working hypothesis.

- Measurement of quantities to be observed and evaluation of actual conditions.

- Modification of engineering to suit actual conditions.

Even though these developments resulted in dramatic improvement in the delivery of environmental remediation work, a lot more had to be done to become the company exemplified in CH2M Hill's mission, vision, and values statements. While CH2M Hill had responded to clients' criteria to be better, cheaper, faster, and safer, the firm had not achieved best, cheapest, fastest, and safest. To meet these demanding internal criteria, processes beyond those implemented on environmental remediation projects were needed. Even to the casual observer, irrespective of the uncomplimentary site cleanup performance data circulating in the media, many instances of duplication of organizational efforts, such as project overview, existed on environmental cleanup sites. On the other hand, some important activities were not sufficiently addressed. Most important, potential risks and uncertainties were not managed consistently, nor was the overall vulnerability of the company managed. This situation led to IPA.

INTEGRATED PERFORMANCE ASSURANCE

The elements missing from the mix of strategies, people, processes, structure, and tools being brought to bear on meeting the DOE and EPA criteria of better, cheaper, faster, and safer were those aspects that distinguish a successful small company from the "also rans."

How IPA addresses the small business criteria differs slightly in different business environments. The perceived value of the IPA concept as a function of company variability is outlined in Appendix A. Three general circumstances are discussed next as examples of how integration of the IPA elements maps into the small business criteria map and meets clients' expectations.

SIMILARITIES OF FUNCTION IN MANAGEMENT SYSTEMS

Industry has traditionally managed its performance assurance functions as separate entities because they employ separate technical disciplines. While this is true, these programs serve a common underlying objective (i.e., performance assurance and risk management); use common approaches to achieve that objective (i.e., activity-specific evaluation, planning, and oversight); and share common success and failure measures (i.e., cost, schedule, violations, and liabilities). With such similarities, additional value and operational effectiveness can be derived from their integration. The magnitude of the potential savings that could be expected from true integration of IPA elements has been estimated to be a minimum of one-third.

REGULATORY ENVIRONMENT AND INTERNATIONAL STANDARDS

Environmental, safety and health, and related regulations are numerous and complex. These primary performance-based regulations are now being supplemented by management system standards, such as ISO 9000 and 14000, that emphasize the incorporation of quality assurance and quality control systems. The emerging regulatory picture is an integrated structure that embodies environmental safety and health protection, combined with quality standards and practices.

The generic benefits of ISO 9000 and 14000 are very similar. Cascio et al. list the following as the major benefits of implementing ISO 14000:

- Enhances a company's ability to trade internationally.

- Enhances a company's ability to understand and communicate internationally on quality and environmental matters.

- Creates an international consensus of quality and environmental management.

- Provides a company with a consistent framework in which to improve its performance in providing products and services.

- Systematizes and integrates quality and environmental management into the overall management to achieve affordable, consistent compliance with applicable requirements.

- Engages all employees in the continuous improvement process.

- Enables cultural change to occur within the implementing organization.

These objectives are very similar to those of IPA and are consistent with the attributes of a small, successful business. For example, a motherboard production facility of a major computer manufacturer decided to become certified to ISO 9000 quality assurance requirements (Smith, 1995). ISO 9000 certification requires well-defined use of process and critical evaluation procedures. By involving the advisory plant safety and industrial hygiene engineer in creating the new procedures, the plant built safety into the work procedures in ways that substantially improved safety statistics. For example, important safety reminders like "wear latex gloves" and "check machine guards" were easily blended into work procedures.

The same actions intended to satisfy quality requirements and ensure that quality motherboards were produced also automatically improved safety and environmental compliance. The result was significant improvement in safety statistics. Employees realized that a safe work environment contributes to both quality of the work and of life. Further reasons for considering ISO involvement in IPA are given in Appendix D.

ISO's Technical Management Board recognizes the need to integrate management standards (Zuckerman 1997). In January 1997, the board recommended that the technical advisory group address the integration of ISO 9000 and ISO 14000 standards. On January 30, the ISO council approved the recommendation. While support for integrating occupational health and safety with the existing ISO management standards is still developing, there is clear direction to blend the quality and environmental management standards.

EFFICIENCY AND COMPETITION

Businesses, as a matter of survival, are becoming intensely competitive. It is therefore essential that they implement cost-effective programs to manage their risks. It is also essential that these programs be reliable; in today's litigious environment, a single failure to perform can lead to complete failure of the business. IPA provides a mechanism to improve cost-effectiveness and reliability by taking advantage of the synergy between risk mitigation disciplines.

REFERENCES

Brown, Stuart M., David R. Lincoln, and William Wallace. (1989). *Application of the Observational Method to Remediation of Hazardous Waste Sites*. Bellevue, WA: CH2M Hill.

Cascio, Joseph, Gayle Woodshed, and Philip Mitchell. (1996). *ISO 14000 Guide*. New York: McGraw-Hill.

CH2M Hill. (1996). *Project Delivery: A System and Process for Benchmark Performance*. Denver: CH2M Hill and Work Systems Associates.

Hesselbein, Frances, Marshall Goldsmith, and Richard Beckhard, eds. (1997). *The Organization of the Future*. San Francisco: Jossey-Bass.

Peck, R. B. (1969). "Advantages and Limitations of the Observational Method in Applied Soil Mechanics." *Geotechnique*, 19. pp. 171–187.

Zuckerman, Amy. (March, 1997). "Uncertain Future for Management System Standards." *Quality Progress*. pp. 21–23.

TWO

COST/BENEFIT ANALYSIS

Critical Business Success Factors for IPA

Understand business competitors and strategic plans

Learn business language

Manage IPA like a business

Merge environmental protection, health and safety, regulatory compliance, and quality assurance into business processes

(adapted from *Integrated Management Systems Update* Vol. 1 No 7 Oct 96)

INTRODUCTION

The IPA concepts of blending common activities to reduce expenses and improve effectiveness can enhance the bottom line of any size and type of business. When these activities become properly integrated into everyday planning and execution, the benefits will accumulate. Because IPA is applied in a performance-based context, it can be tailored to meet a range of business objectives in a variety of settings. Not only will the IPA concepts work in all business areas, but also the degree to which IPA is implemented can be matched to the specific company.

The objective of this chapter is to give the reader the framework necessary to answer the question, "What is the net benefit of IPA for my company?" The three keys to this question are an understanding of the general IPA approach, of the type and size of costs involved in IPA implementation, and of the type and size of benefits that can accrue from implementing IPA.

This chapter begins with a brief discussion of the IPA process and its relationship to overall risk management. The level and degree of IPA implementation are explained and illustrated by two surveys on value and implementation. Following this examination of IPA versatility, an analysis of IPA costs is presented. This discussion offers a cost-estimating framework and addresses both the costs that can be averted through the application of IPA and the expenditures to be anticipated in its implementation. Next, the benefits of IPA are presented. The final section combines the costs and the benefits into a cost/benefit discussion and suggests a way to optimize the level of IPA that might be selected for implementation by any company, based on its specific needs and business setting.

IPA PROCESS AND RELATIONSHIPS

IPA is the integrated management and execution of regulatory compliance (RC), environmental protection (EP), quality assurance (QA), and human health and safety (H&S). Other technical disciplines may be included or substituted, but the emphasis is on these four elements. The best method to achieve the desired level of integration of these elements is shown in Exhibit 2-1.

A "reward/recover" element has been added to the traditional plan/do/check/act cycle. On performance-based contracts, the response normally goes well beyond the "fix the problem" component usually associated with the "act" element. On

EXHIBIT 2–1. THE IPA/DEMING CYCLE PROCESS

these contracts, whether the job went well or not so well, significant effort is involved in evaluating outcome vis-à-vis performance measures and metrics. The evaluation is conducted to determine the proportion of available fee pool to be awarded on the basis of work done. If the work has gone well, there may be some provision for passing rewards down to workers who delivered the outcomes. If the work did not go well, and gross errors such as negligence, endangerment, and nonconformances occurred, policy may call for disciplinary personnel actions. Under the same set of circumstances, financial penalties may be assessed by the customer.

Work is first planned in detail, with involvement of both management and workers who will be responsible for proper IPA execution. This enables the incorporation of only necessary and sufficient requirements in the work plan and makes way for a graded application. The work is then executed according to the plan and is checked for consistency with the expected performance measures and outcome. If the work meets all expectations, management acts to reward the effort. If the work does not meet all expectations, management acts to recover from any shortcomings of the effort. This IPA process, which is similar to the familiar Deming cycle, is consistent with existing models for best management practice.

The key factor in the IPA context is to include all four of the IPA program elements simultaneously. This contrasts with the historical approach, in which all four IPA elements may have been addressed, but with fragmented expectations and, most likely, different management teams and organizational components.

Exhibit 2-2 shows the relationship of IPA to a total risk management strategy. Risk management is made up of many components. As used here, IPA envelops elements that are technical in nature like environmental protection, human health and safety, regulatory compliance, and quality assurance as well as others in specific instances. Nontechnical elements may include contracts, finance, legal, and many others. In the intersection of IPA and applicable nontechnical elements, risk management resides. It is from this powerful relationship with other risk management elements that the IPA elements derive a total value that is greater than the sum of the individual elemental values. It is also from this synergistic relationship that the full spectrum of risk management benefits arises.

IPA IMPLEMENTATION AND VALUE

Based on business-specific conditions, tailored IPA will encompass only applicable performance elements. For example, IPA for a business that provides design services will include only regulatory compliance and quality assurance. Manufacturing operations, however, can benefit from an IPA function that encompasses all four performance assurance elements.

Exhibit 2–2. Relationship of IPA to Risk Management

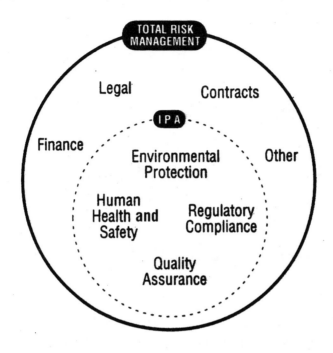

Businesses often complete major programmatic changes in stages. A companywide change may proceed slowly, phased in over months or years, or the company's divisions, plants, or other business units could rapidly adopt the change at one time. Although some companies may stop after finishing only a portion of the implementation plan, the level and degree of implementation of IPA are intended to be based on the initial vision. The level of IPA implementation combines the number of program elements (i.e., QA, H&S, RC, and EP) actually integrated with the depth of integration (i.e., how far down the organization the integration extends as a daily working reality). The degree of integration is a combination of the depth and breadth (i.e., how much of the company is involved in the integration), measured by the number of organizational units. Exhibit 2-3 shows these relationships.

EXHIBIT 2–3. DEGREE OF IPA IMPLEMENTATION

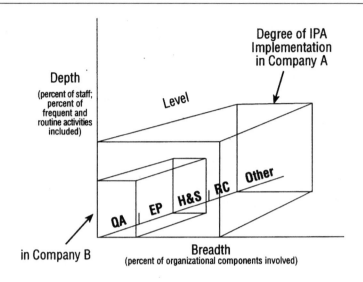

The degree and level of implementation of IPA a company chooses will be affected by a variety of factors. The right amount of IPA may be difficult to judge in advance. Achieving a balance between getting the most benefit from your investment and sufficient expenditure of resources to create a viable program is a reasonable target. Market entrance or government requirements, a potential competitive advantage, available funding, funding and investment strategies, business culture, and middle management attitudes are all possible factors to consider when planning your IPA program. The company's strategic business plan (Kaplan and Norton 1992) provides an excellent framework for IPA implementation planning and is a source of insight into these factors.

IPA IMPLEMENTATION SURVEY

Two surveys were conducted to examine the value of IPA and the level and degree of implementation. The internal survey asked CH2M Hill's client service managers about the real or perceived value of IPA to their clients and business applications.

The results of this survey are summarized in Appendix A. Also, a broad survey (Appendix F) of various firms gauged the current implementation of IPA.

Consulting firms, manufacturers, hospitals, Internet companies, biotechnology firms, utilities, timber and paper product companies, petrochemical firms, government organizations, food and agribusinesses all potentially can benefit from IPA. About 40 such small, large, national, or international organizations in Europe and the United States were asked about their ongoing or planned IPA activities. Additional information published on the Internet by firms, associations, and standards setting organizations supplemented the surveys.

About half of the companies responded. As shown in Exhibit 2-4, the responses fell into four areas:

- Are not integrated or unsure what it means.

- Are somewhat integrated.

- Are in the process of major integration or are integrated.

- Know of another company that is better integrated.

No company that had integrated completely or partially had a full set of experiences that they wished to relate.

In the United States, it appears that integration of performance assurance functions is neither widespread nor well recognized. Only a few of the companies contacted are actively pursuing integration. Most respondents emphasize that one of the IPA elements is integrated with processing operations. The companies that have integrated are large, with global or at least multinational components. They may have facilities located around the world, sell internationally, or both. These companies see a competitive benefit that transcends mere compliance. A more mature company with a broader perspective can usually see more diffuse benefits—that is, although the cost savings may not be easily quantified, the benefits do accumulate and will have a measurable impact.

The trend toward global markets, the European Union, and increased international trade agreements has prompted a broad

EXHIBIT 2–4. IMPLEMENTATION SURVEY RESPONSES

Implementation Survey Responses	
My company is:	
not integrated or unsure what it means	65%
somewhat integrated	20%
in the process of major integration or is integrated	15%
We know of another company that is better integrated	10%

cross-section of companies to adopt international consensus standards such as ISO 9000 and 14000. The ISO 14000 continuous improvement model includes a principle for full integration of the environmental program with health and safety, quality, finance, business planning, and other essential management processes. Implementation of these standards can be used to drive improvements in business performance.

The survey also revealed a European influence, primarily emphasizing cultural differences and the ISO standards. However, in early 1997, after an open workshop on the subject, the ISO decided not to initiate an occupational health and safety (OH&S) management system. While a global, concerted effort to officially integrate safety with quality and environmental issues appears to have diminished, it is still emphasized in Europe. For example, a Dutch firm teaches companies to accommodate quality, health and safety, and environmental issues within a single practice-oriented management system.

The survey revealed a general relationship between awareness and implementation of IPA, as Exhibit 2-5 shows. The larger companies have the greater knowledge and, usually, degree of integration. Consulting firms are an exception, in that while usually small, they have a great deal of knowledge about integration of performance assurance functions. For example, one international consulting firm offers help in designing and implementing a quality-based, environmental, health and safety organization that is fully integrated with business objectives.

EXHIBIT 2–5. IMPLEMENTATION SURVEY RESULT

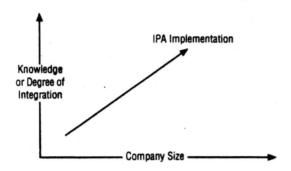

In Exhibit 2-5, degree of integration means primarily the scope—that is, how many program elements are integrated and the segments of the company (i.e., number of plants or divisions) that are involved, not the length of time integration has existed or what organizational levels within the company are integrated. Within a business component, integration appears to involve all organizational levels, components, and processes, or none.

Most respondents do not appear to recognize that the broader or generic concept of integration, such as that achieved with high-performance teams, can yield companywide improvements. Instead, most seem to focus on merging one organizational element (one stovepipe) with another. As a result, any cost-driven managers immediately look for reduced overhead expenses.

The situation represented in Exhibit 2-5 should not be construed to indicate that integration is only for large, multinational companies. Rather, it illustrates that the best companies, also in global competition, have recognized the benefits of integration. The smaller companies need effective performance programs, too, perhaps even more so. Smaller companies, although with shallower pockets, may be more volatile and subject to more risk than larger organizations. The challenge for smaller companies is to understand that they can reap the benefits of integration with incremental investment in systematizing their processes. Often the smaller business is already somewhat integrated, but just does not recognize it.

Because the concepts are the same, IPA integration is implemented much the same in a small business as in a large one, and because small businesses often compete with much larger companies, it is especially important to offer their clients value not found with the larger companies. A well-planned and executed integration effort, plus the cost associated with it, is actually an investment in the company. The size of the firm should not be a consideration when deciding about whether to integrate performance programs.

IPA VALUE SURVEY

To show the value of IPA to a wide variety of companies (with different sizes, business objectives, and business settings), 12 diverse business groups that represent some of CH2M Hill's core clients, large and small, were surveyed (Appendix A). The complete list includes companies of all sizes in all business sectors, but major clients manufacture chemicals, pharmaceuticals, textiles and fibers, plastics, rubber, and aerospace and other transportation equipment. Other large clients find, refine, transport, and market petroleum products. Major service clients are in printing, communications, electric and gas utilities, and telecommunications. The geographical scope of business operations ranges from large multinational to small foreign and domestic operations. The list also includes large and small municipalities and government groups, both foreign and domestic.

The CH2M Hill program owners for each of these 12 business group practices were asked to rate the importance of the four IPA elements to conducting business and the importance of having a fully implemented IPA process for projects.

The results are shown in Exhibit 2-6. More than half of all responses fall into the "very high" category. There is no discernible correlation between the responses and the sizes of the businesses. Nearly all of the remaining responses are in the

EXHIBIT 2-6. BUSINESS GROUPS THAT VALUE IPA

Business Group	Importance of IPA
Chemical/Petroleum	High
Environmental Management and Compliance	High
Environmental Restoration	Very High
Facility Operations	High
Industrial Waste Management	High
Manufacturing, Industrials, and Technology	High
Risk and Ecosystem Management	High
Transportation Infrastructure	Medium
Utilities	Medium
Wastewater Collection and Treatment	Medium
Water Resources	Medium
Water Treatment and Supply	Medium

Choices were: None, Low, Medium, High, and Very High

"high" category. The number of "high" and "very high" entries over the variety of business types and sizes illustrates the potential utility of the IPA approach in the minds of the program owners and their clients.

The "medium" responses cluster with the groups whose clients are mostly public, municipal, or government agencies. Deregulation has injected some new considerations for some of these businesses, but most of them have existed and continue to exist in relatively stable environments. Although cost management is usually stressed by such agencies, the amount of competition they typically face is lower than for the private sector businesses. This supports the statements by some respondents in the implementation survey that IPA not only provides a competitive edge now, but is necessary for continued prosperity in the near future.

IMPLEMENTATION COSTS

Experience has shown that costs associated with the implementation of an IPA function can be more than offset by the long-term benefits to the business, not the least of which is cost savings. There is a time factor to the costs as well, as some parts are changed one year, some in later years. Since time is money, an approach to justifying the expenses of IPA may well benefit from investment-type thinking. Using whatever concept your company favors (i.e., payback period, internal rate of return, or net present value) may help win over the chief financial officer or any cost-driven managers (Higgins 1995; Brealey and Myers 1991).

Initiating an IPA program, or accounting for an ongoing one, does have an effect on the income statement. However, the entries attributable to only IPA will be hard to spot on a typical consolidated income statement. An income statement segmented for components of a business might show the entries more readily.

IPA and the programs it replaces cost the company—that is, they show up as an expense. There may be an initial expense to start the IPA program, too. Compared to traditional compliance programs, however, IPA may cost less, may help sell more products or services, and may have some recoverable costs. If the allocation of IPA costs is questioned, it is worthwhile to look carefully at what costs will actually continue if the allocation changes or if IPA funding is reduced.

Often all costs of IPA activities will show up as overhead and be included with the selling expenses or the general and administrative expenses. Either way, the initial impact of accounting for IPA on the income statement is to decrease the net income, with the typical result of focusing attention on cutting the costs of IPA.

Methods such as activity-based costing (ABC) or activity-based management (ABM) can help identify the sources of compliance costs and assign them to billable services and products (Hilton 1994). A major consulting firm reported that one of their clients, a major pharmaceutical company, recently saved more than $70 million by redesigning its compliance functions, reducing waste, and using less energy.

Extraordinary items, restructuring charges, and write-downs are entries on balance sheets that summarize occasional, costly events. An acute, companywide IPA initiative may qualify as one of these. The tax implications, market response, and executive bonus structure should be pondered before using these labels on such an event.

You should compare a future income statement with IPA to the present one without IPA to judge the net effect. Although initiating IPA creates expenses unmatched by revenues (for that particular accounting period), once in place, an integrated system is designed to reduce costs. For example, the cost of audits will likely decrease, and those of maintaining separate programs (e.g., documentation, labor, and supplies) should go down. These are all included with the expenses on the income statement. So trading the costs of traditional compliance programs for the costs of IPA is a net gain if the IPA activities cost less—or if there is some added value that allows you to increase prices or sales. Whereas traditional cost accounting methods may imperil an IPA project, an activity-based accounting process may show a very different result.

Measuring your performance is vital to a successful IPA program. Associated costs can be minimized or even reduced from current levels if you carefully choose your metrics and design your management information system (Eccles 1991). Even integrating nothing but the metrics and reporting system for the IPA performance elements should achieve some cost savings.

Each business will have its own solution to funding integration activities. The owners of a very small business will likely work more unpaid hours. Other businesses may combine a plan of small steps coupled with pricing strategies to accomplish their goal. This will be more effective if customers see added value for any higher prices. Some companies may focus on reducing or shifting costs. Still others may be able to fund the activities through financing, especially if they are following a written strategic plan. A lot of businesses will simply write a list of activities and fund only those with the highest priority or perceived benefits. This last solution may be acceptable for a survival mode, but not for a healthy growth strategy.

COST ELEMENTS OF IPA

The first objective of this section is to identify the major elements that have to be addressed to evaluate the costs of implementing an IPA function and determine which of those might be averted. The second is to put them into a cost-estimating framework, combined with a benefit analysis method, and easily applied to specific cases to answer the question, "What is the net benefit of IPA for my company?"

Objectives must be developed and communicated, organizational realignments and consolidation must be accomplished, management systems must be merged, and training must be provided. Implementing an IPA function requires an IPA process, a strategy, an organizational structure, people, and tools. Several workable alternatives exist for implementing strategies. Outsourcing functions, or subfunctions, may be an especially attractive alternative for small businesses with less than full-time need for certain technical specialists or subject matter experts; however, the IPA function champion, implementers, and director should almost always be employees of the implementing organization. The alternative emphasized here, is implementing IPA with existing in-house resources. To maximize successful implementation, it should be planned, resourced, scheduled, and managed as a project.

Once all of the essential resources are accounted for, using readily available computer software, it is possible to create a process flow for resource loading the project and estimating the associated costs. Such a flow diagram is instrumental in ensuring a logical project plan and scheduling, resource loading, and rolling out the IPA implementation process. If the implementation process is well structured, it can also be the source of a number of performance indicators and metrics to be applied to both the program and the individuals responsible for its maturation and implementation.

Exhibit 2-7 is a cost-estimating worksheet. It contains both fixed and operational costs for both the startup and initial operational phase of the sample IPA program, divided into develop-

Exhibit 2-7. Summary of Implementation Hours

	Business Group	Regional Management	Regional Technology	Regional Support	Corporate IPA	Corporate Other	Total
Culture Change/Staff Acceptance							
Policies and Programs	350	50	0	285	1,665	1,000	3,350
Awareness Education							
Reinforcement	0	0	0	215	650	135	1,000
Senior Regional Staff Network	0	0	0	40	200	0	240
Process Development/Implementation							
S&RM Checklist Processes and Database	300	100	675	100	1,100	475	2,750
Training							
Lessons Learned Database	0	0	400	100	750	125	1,375
Maintenance	150	0	50	375	775	225	1,575
Total Hours	800	150	1,125	1,115	5,140	1,960	10,290

ment, tools, training, and maintenance categories. The data shown are in units of hours, so that readers can input their own appropriate charge-out rate and make the analysis match their specific situation. A charge-out rate of $50 per hour has been assumed to make the mathematics simple for illustration purposes. The hours used in the sample program are based on experiences with implementing IPA in a large, multinational service business with several thousand employees.

Upper estimates of the principal cost elements are as follows:

- Cultural change/staff acceptance – 5,000 hours — $250,000.
- Process development/implementation – 5,000 hours — $250,000.
- Annual maintenance (verification and assessment) – 2,000 hours — $100,000.

This gives a total cost of $600,000 for 12,000 hours expended.

Because the cost elements that all businesses use are essentially the same, this approach is effective for developing cost estimates for drastically different types of businesses. In addition, IPA is demonstrably cost-effective for types of businesses that encompass all, or most, of the IPA elements. This is because the integrated management approach used in IPA brings most of the key attributes at the same fixed cost that would be expended for a single attribute, if all IPA elements were implemented independently. Even though this characteristic of IPA may make it possible for larger companies to gain more from their investment, in the authors' experience, even application at the small project level is more cost-effective than the segmented approach. The percentage of benefits per dollar invested may even be greater than for larger applications.

AVERTED COSTS

Exhibit 2-8 illustrates the magnitude of the 1966 cost risks that a company can run in the regulatory compliance area only (U.S. EPA 1996). Also included are the potential 1996 fines for Price Anderson Amendments Act violations, as defined in the Act. Similar data show that many companies are willing to pay these fines and penalties without contesting them because the litigation costs can be orders of magnitude higher than the fines themselves. The order of magnitude of these assessments does not, in general, depend on the type of business or the regulator with jurisdiction over that business sector. It may, however, depend significantly on the specific characteristics of a company and the size of a company's involvement in the sector, as reflected by its annual revenue.

In general, other than IPA implementation, costs can be quantified only in the context of a specific business. For purposes of illustration later in this section, the following order of magnitude cost estimates have been attributed to not having an IPA program in place:

- Loss of clients–$10,000,000
- Litigation costs–$1,000,000
- Fines/penalties–$100,000
- Insurance premiums–$10,000

Exhibit 2-8. Compliance Risks

	Highest Proposed Penalty	Total Penalties Assessed in 1996
CERCLA[1]	$100,000	$145,000
CAA[2]	$1,300,000	$2,498,367
CWA[3]	$145,000	$1,897,200
EPCRA[4]	$124,135	$513,555
FIFRA[5]	$16,000	$23,000
RCRA[6]	$1,212,433	$2,249,044
TSCA[7]	$200,000	$732,375
SDWA[8]	$20,000	$20,000

[1] Comprehensive Environmental Response, Compensation and Liability Act
[2] Clean Air Act
[3] Clean Water Act
[4] Emergency Planning and Community Right-to-Know Act
[5] Federal Insecticide, Fungicide, and Rodenticide Act
[6] Resource Conservation and Recovery Act
[7] Toxic Substances Control Act
[8] Safe Drinking Water Act

BENEFITS

In addition to cost savings and averting major cost risks, adopting an IPA approach to risk management provides a range of performance benefits. For example, the compliance function identifies the regulations and requirements for a given activity. The quality assurance function is driven by these as well as more customer-specific requirements. Integrating the compliance and quality assurance functions ensures that the most appropriate, cost-effective approach level is applied for quality assurance. The quality assurance function can bring improved discipline of implementation to the safety and health function. The integration of these two results in a reduction of risks associated with performing hazardous operations. Further, the integration of safety and health with the compliance function provides greater assurance that stakeholder concerns will be satisfied.

Hard data on benefits such as cost savings or increased market share that are also publishable are difficult to find. Respondents in the implementation survey either did not wish to reveal such information or, more commonly, had not been

EXHIBIT 2-9. IPA BENEFITS

Teamwork versus after-the-fact integration.

More precise line management accountability/responsibility/authorities.

More concise communication of roles/responsibilities.

Improved overall organizational productivity.

Increased consistency across disciplinary boundaries.

Removal of duplication of effort.

Increased opportunity to use necessary, sufficient, and graded approaches across disciplines.

Simplified project planning process.

running their IPA programs long enough to accumulate hard data on such benefits. Most respondents could identify areas where costs are being reduced but did not yet have specific figures. Although this situation may not satisfy the cost-driven manager who is worried about next quarter's income statement, it is a necessary step for those who would move into the uncharted future and stay ahead of the competition.

Exhibit 2-9 lists the most common IPA implementation benefits cited by users of the approach. These benefits tend to be more focused on cost savings than on cost avoidance, although the latter tend to have much greater value than the former. This is also true when the classical definition of risk (consequence times probability of occurrence) is used in the analysis.

Cost savings can accrue in two general areas that are often accounted for as overhead. Even using traditional accounting methods, the IPA program should have lower costs than the once separate program elements, principally because of the elimination of duplicated effort. However, the thorough examination of a company's internal business process that happens with the implementation of IPA can often show less apparent ways to reduce costs. Improving and combining metrics and reporting systems, or removing ineffective measures, can reduce the effort spent on these resource-consuming activities. Unexpected benefits are also attributed to the synergistic nature of the IPA process. Real margin eaters, like waste disposal costs, can often be reduced when different staffs collaborate through the IPA process. For example, a small firm that produces electric motors now has lower costs for raw materials, waste treatment, and energy because of the integration of purchasing, safety, and quality assurance.

Market Value

A nontangible asset (e.g., technical expertise or a trademark) can have real value to a company and show up on the balance sheet; that is, the nontangible asset will have a book value, like Coca-Cola's logo. An IPA program will likely not add book value, but if the market thinks IPA adds value to your company, that added value will be reflected in the price per share of your stock, your bond rating, or your ability to secure a loan. If clients (a subset of the market) think your having IPA adds value, the number or dollar value of sales may increase. Your market share may go up, too, which in turn should increase your market value.

If IPA adds market value, your customers should be willing to pay a higher price for your products or services. In some situations, IPA may be almost a requirement for entry into a market, especially the European Union. In this case, IPA adds no direct value because it is an expected part of doing business, but it does expand your market opportunities.

COST OPTIMIZATION

Given that the benefits of the IPA approach are easily identified for any specific set of business circumstances and the costs of IPA implementation are easily estimated, one might ask, "Can the benefits be optimized to cost?" The answer is definitely yes. Relevant data presented earlier in this section are used to make this optimization with the following assumptions:

- Accomplishment of the development portion of IPA will avoid the loss of clients.

EXHIBIT 2–10. COSTS OF POTENTIAL LOSSES

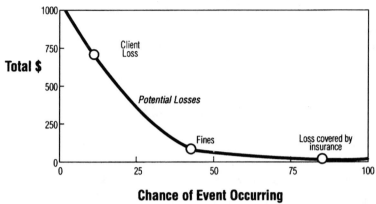

Chance of Event Occurring

- Accomplishment of development and tools and training will avoid litigation costs.

- Accomplishment of development, tools and training, and maintenance will avoid fines and penalties.

OPTIMIZATION

Exhibit 2-10 shows a plot of the dollar value lost due to unfavorable events that have a chance of happening. These data are taken from the cost risks shown in Exhibit 2-8.

Exhibit 2-11 shows the cost of the IPA program as a function of completion. The curves in Exhibit 2-10 and Exhibit 2-11 are combined (with an adjustment for scale) in the plot shown in Exhibit 2-12. Exhibit 2-12 illustrates the total cost to avoid each of the events through an effective IPA program. Per the assumptions stated in the previous section, spending the total $600,000 will result in avoidance of the highest cost events. Spending $500,000 (not the $100,000 for maintenance) will result in attaining a risk level that avoids all but the smallest and least expensive events.

When both curves are plotted, they intersect at a risk level associated with most litigation costs and a total cost level around $400,000. To simplify the optimization process, many

EXHIBIT 2–11. IPA BUDGET VERSUS COMPLETION

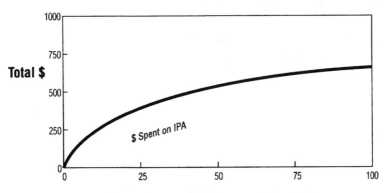

Percentage of IPA Program Completion

use this as the optimal point. This would indicate that the program designers in the example have either found a higher risk level unacceptable and have opted to spend beyond the optimum cost, or that the program has not been subjected to the optimization process.

The true optimum point, however, is represented where the sum of curves is at a minimum. This minimum can be verified graphically by examining Exhibit 2-12. Therefore, at this

EXHIBIT 2–12. IPA OPTIMIZATION

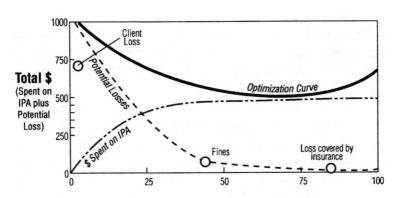

**Percent of IPA Program Completion
or Chance of Loss Occurring**

level of accuracy, the proposed program, estimated to cost $600,000, is deemed to be optimum.

The recommended use of this optimization method is to go through the process, as it has been described. Then, based on the results, reassess the allocation of cost resources to achieve the desired level of risk for the optimal expenditure of financial resources. In many cases, based on an increased sensitivity of the results to the input assumptions, these assumptions can be refined and often assist in this fine-tuning process.

There may be cases when the potential loss curve appears to be too steep relative to the cost curve for implementing IPA, and the intersection point occurs at very low values of risk level and/or very high avoidance cost values. This indicates that one can expect very inefficient reduction of risk. Even at large expenditures for risk reduction, there are two possible explanations for this phenomenon. First, the cost of the risk levels could be grossly overestimated and should be reexamined. Second, the risk reduction remedies that have been included are ineffective in reducing risk in a cost-efficient way and should be reexamined for possible replacement with more effective mitigating measures. On a specific project, this situation may require not making a bid on this work.

In some cases, no optimal level appears because the potential loss curve is too flat relative to the IPA cost curve. Either the selected risk mitigation measures are very effective, or one might reassess the accuracy of the cost estimates included in both curves to make sure of their accuracy. If the cost estimates are accurate, the risk mitigation system in the optimization analysis is highly effective in attaining the objectives of the analyst.

With this level of understanding of the IPA approach and definition, the costs involved in IPA implementation and their quantification, and the benefits that can accrue from IPA and their quantification, one should be able to tailor the methods discussed to a specific set of circumstances. Then one can answer the question, "Is there a net benefit from IPA for my company?"

CONCLUSION

Although many of the details of the planning, implementation, and application of the IPA approach remain to be developed in detail in the following sections, several conclusions can be drawn at this point. First, on the basis of the prevailing management theory (CH2M Hill 1996), current business pressures, and input from practicing management personnel, IPA is a strategy whose time has come. It is effective in supporting the business goals of becoming more efficient, and more competitive, organizations. Second, IPA has widespread applicability over the spectrum of business types, sizes, and settings. Third, it is feasible to implement IPA for most types of companies, in a cost-effective, if not an optimal, way. Last, properly done, IPA can result in great benefits in revenue generation and cost avoidance.

Integration efforts can benefit from the lessons learned by those companies that embraced total quality management in the early and mid-1980s. A number of the companies that won the Malcolm Baldrige National Quality Award later experienced financial difficulties. It seems that pursuing quality for its own sake drove costs higher than clients could afford and often did not add value (i.e., it added activities that were unimportant to or unappreciated by clients). Narrowly defined quality objectives that emphasized quality and not management were one major reason for the failure of these programs and companies.

EP and H&S issues can have significant impacts on financial performance, growth, and global market share. Typical impacts include compliance costs, project or product delays, costs of legal defenses, and access to financing. Integration is a systematic way of reducing impacts that address all aspects of a business: operations, products, and services.

REFERENCES

Brealey, Richard A., and Stewart C. Myers. (1991). *Principles of Corporate Finance*, 4th Ed. New York: McGraw-Hill.

Capezio, Peter, and Debra Morehouse. (1995). *Taking the Mystery Out of TQM*. Franklin Lakes, NJ: Career Press.

CEEM Information Services. (October 1996). *Integrated Management Systems Update*, Vol. 1, No. 7.

CH2M Hill and Work Systems Associates, Inc. (1996). *Project Delivery—A System and Process for Benchmark Performance*. Denver.

Deming, W. Edwards. (1950). Seminar. Japan.

Eccles, Robert G. (January-February 1991). "The Performance Measurement Manifesto." *Harvard Business Review*.

Higgins, Robert C. (1995). *Analysis for Financial Management*, 4th Ed. Chicago: Irwin.

Hilton, Ronald W. (1994). *Managerial Accounting*, 2nd Ed. New York: McGraw-Hill.

Kaplan, Robert S., and David P. Norton. (January-February 1992). "The Balanced Scorecard—Measures that Drive Performance." *Harvard Business Review*.

U.S. EPA. (1996). *Enforcement Docket System*. Seattle: U.S. Environmental Protection Agency Database.

THREE

IMPLEMENTATION PLANNING

Implementing an IPA function, and integrating it with your company's other management systems, produces an array of positive benefits. As discussed in chapters 1 and 2, these include increased business opportunities, enhanced loss prevention, and reduced insurance costs. It is also an important step toward achieving the attributes of a highly successful enterprise. If your organization is considering ISO 9000/14000 quality and environmental management systems (Q/EMS), implementation of an IPA organization and function will greatly enhance and facilitate development of an ISO-conforming QMS and/or EMS.

Despite these pluses, implementing an IPA function introduces a number of changes, and, because of these, it may be met with resistance. If this happens, your success will depend on having a detailed and well-conceived approach, the necessary resources, and a rational schedule. In other words, you need a plan.

We recommend applying a project approach to planning and managing your IPA function, then integrating that function throughout your organization. A project approach is based on tangible discrete objectives, in specific time frames, using quantitative resources (i.e., the team will accomplish this by this specific date, for this specific amount of resources). A project approach will also be more salable to management, not to mention much easier for you to manage.

GROUNDWORK

The best-laid plans can still go astray without the proper groundwork. Management support and commitment must be obtained, a champion must be identified, an effective implementation team must be established, and clear, explicit mission and policy statements must be developed and communicated throughout your company. Taking these steps before putting your IPA implementation plan into effect can greatly improve your effectiveness and ultimate success. Each of these elements is discussed in the following sections.

MANAGEMENT SUPPORT

Gaining management support is a required element of your planning process. Management support from the top down is vital, but it must be matched by support from the bottom up and the middle out. Management support at all levels of the organization not only reaffirms your company's endorsement of the IPA initiative, but it also serves to prevent (or overcome) pockets of resistance within your company.

Passive support is not enough. Management's support must be active and provide leadership. Only in small hierarchical organizations will you be able to get the job done on your own with no more than a statement (i.e., an edict) of management support. Leadership occurs when your management team takes a proactive role in the process, helping you communicate the key messages to staff, asking questions within the organization, and looking for opportunities to integrate IPA within operational activities. True integration of the IPA function within your company's management systems and across your operations requires acceptance by all staff, and an effective plan must incorporate management leadership activities.

The example mission and policy statement discussed in a later section is framed on the foundation of safety, health, and environmental protection (central objectives of the four IPA functions) as core values for your company. Core values, to be truly persuasive in guiding company actions and operations, must also be pervasive (core values are the ones you fall back on during adversity). In most organizations, this involves some degree of culture change, which is a key objective for the communications element of your implementation plan.

Management and staff endorsement is facilitated by showing the business (and personal) value added as a result of an effective IPA program as well as the direct links between IPA and the company's mission and vision. Example presentations to different levels of management are provided in Appendix G. Appendix H presents three sample training presentations that were used at CH2M Hill to acquaint various groups with IPA.

The current regulatory climate ensures that management, once properly acquainted with the risk involved in operations under its control, will see the corporate and personal advantage of an effective IPA program. Appendix B provides selected case histories that illustrate the importance of an IPA function to effective risk management.

A CHAMPION

Experience shows that without a champion to continuously press for a viable IPA program, movement will be slow to nonexistent. Absent a catastrophe, the tendency is to concentrate on short-term objectives and ignore risk management (e.g., pay attention to the squeaky wheel and delay preventive maintenance elsewhere). Consequently, one of the first steps toward implementing your program is to identify the IPA champion. That person may or may not have credentials in one or more of the disciplines comprising IPA but, most importantly, must have personal attributes of persistence, good communication skills, technical knowledge of likely corporate risks, and access to (and credibility with) top levels of management. Your job will be to work closely with this champion in developing your implementation plan and identifying the most effective information and resources for gaining endorsement of your IPA initiative within your company.

IMPLEMENTATION TEAM

The composition of the implementation team is an important consideration during preparation for the planning effort. Appropriate staffing of the team by individuals from across the company ensures that the right interests are represented by individuals who are trusted and respected. This contributes to endorsement of both the implementation process and the final outcome.

The team should represent a cross-section of the organization and include representatives from operations (customer) groups in addition to members of performance assurance organizations. Your ultimate objective is for performance assurance measures to be integrated into work processes such that operational activities contribute directly to performance assurance. The credibility of the implementation process and the resulting IPA organization and systems will be degraded without participation from within operations groups.

MISSION AND POLICY STATEMENT

Relating IPA to your organization's mission and vision is an important precursor to the planning process as well as a minimum requirement for gaining management support. Your company's mission should keep energies focused on value-added activities, while vision communicates the culture that helps ensure that day-to-day behaviors are consistent with the organizational mission. This produces a cohesive group of behaviors and activities, much in contrast to the historical command and control approach.

Policy statements clearly articulating the core values associated with IPA and their relationship to your company's mission should be drafted and presented to your company's executive management, preferably by your champion. Exhibit 3-1 presents a sample policy statement. The value of a clear and direct policy statement (in this case, one that drives the IPA process) cannot be underestimated. It provides essential focus and a reference point for organizational alignment.

The IPA program mission statement should also be developed so that it completes the linkage. As shown in Exhibit 3-2, the links must be clear and explicit between the company mission and vision, performance policy, and IPA program mission. Sample IPA program mission, goals, and objectives are provided in Exhibit 3-3.

IMPLEMENTATION PLAN

A project approach to developing an implementation plan involves identification of specific tasks and subtasks, with finite schedules, objective deliverables, and specific budgets. The top-level tasks that we recommend for inclusion in your implementation plan (based on our experience as well as that of others) are presented and discussed in the sections that follow. An excellent discussion of planning processes is found in *Quality Centered Strategic Planning* (Dew, 1997).

Economic benefits have led many firms to outsource selected business functions and subfunctions. Outsourcing components of an IPA function (e.g., environmental compliance) may be attractive for both small and large businesses that lack certain technical specialists. Almost always, however, the IPA function champion, implementers, and director should be held within the implementing organization. The strategy discussed here is based on implementation of an IPA function with existing in-house resources.

EXHIBIT 3-1. SAMPLE POLICY STATEMENT

It is this company's policy to be an industry leader in safety, health, and environmental protection performance throughout our operations. We will fulfill the expectations of our clients, staff, and community through safe, innovative, and environmentally sound practices in all our business activities. The following principles will be followed to establish and maintain safety, health, and environmental protection as core values and to create a work place that encourages participation from all staff:

- Management will supply the leadership for development of programs and practices that fully implement this policy and commits the firm's resources to the conduct of an appropriate, firmwide staff awareness education.

- We will consistently reinforce the value and importance of safety, health, and environmental protection to our clients, the firm, and our staff though effective use of corporate, regional, and local communications.

- We will integrate safety and health, environmental protection, and quality assurance programs to optimize effectiveness and to enhance the value added to our operations.

- We will reduce risks to human health and the environment by systematically identifying, evaluating, and where necessary, mitigating hazards associated with our business and project activities.

- We will develop metrics as effective indicators of our safety, health, environmental protection, and quality process performance and will regularly assess and report on that performance.

- We will comply with all federal, state, and local regulations.

- We will hold all staff accountable for their role in safety, health, and environmental protection and will appropriately reward positive practices and penalize negative practices.

- We will proactively seek lessons learned from our activities and the activities of others; use those lessons to identify opportunities for safety, health, and environmental protection performance improvement; and assign high priority to performance improvement when allocating resources.

EXHIBIT 3–2. MISSION, VISION, AND IPA

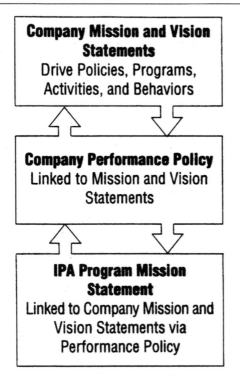

APPROACH OR STRATEGY

There are many ways to implement change. For simplicity, let us consider the extremes. One approach is for management to drop the bomb and make the change all at once with a "starburst." The other extreme involves making small incremental changes in many areas that gradually lead to an overall change. Of course there is infinite variation in between.

Your approach depends on your analysis of what will work best for your organization. What factors are important in this analysis? The matrix in Exhibit 3-4 identifies issues to consider and shows how they may influence whether you lean toward the drop-the-bomb or the incremental approach.

There is merit to going with the flow and taking advantage of the path of least resistance. Recognizing exactly what that

EXHIBIT 3–3. IPA MISSION, GOAL, AND OBJECTIVES

Mission:

Excellence in regulatory compliance, environmental protection, health and safety, and quality assurance throughout our company's business operations and projects.

Goal:

We will ensure that necessary and sufficient regulatory compliance, environmental protection, health and safety (H&S), quality assurance (QA), and risk management planning are included in our company's internal business processes and external client projects and that performance assurance functions are implemented in an integrated manner that enhances their cost-effectiveness and achieves added value for our company and our clients.

As the terms are used here, regulatory compliance means adherence to the provisions of applicable laws. Environmental protection involves engineering, administrative, and preventive measures to preclude environmental impacts.

Objectives:

Deliver risk evaluation/decision process services associated with bid/ no-bid decisions to the business development and planning managers (BD&PMs).

Deliver risk management and H&S, QA, environmental protection, and compliance planning services during project startup to project managers (PMs) in support of the project delivery managers and their implementation of the project delivery process.

Deliver H&S, QA, environmental protection, and compliance services to PMs during project execution.

Deliver IPA training to regional project staff, enabling them to provide effective project-specific H&S and QA services to PMs during project execution.

Delivery H&S training and medical monitoring services to regional project staff that enable them to perform project-specific work assignments safely and in full compliance with applicable federal, state, and local regulations.

Develop and disseminate information and deliver training throughout the firm that will foster a "performance excellence" culture.

Develop and maintain cost-effective regulatory compliance, environmental protection, health and safety, and quality assurance expertise, resources, and systems necessary to achieve the program mission, goals, and objectives, consistent with the highest professional standards.

Develop firmwide review and follow-up processes to ensure that IPA is being implemented properly and effectively.

EXHIBIT 3-4. APPROACH CONSIDERATIONS

Factor	Starburst Approach	Incremental Approach	Why
Size	Small	Large	Logistics of communicating and "turning the battle-ship" argue for an incremental approach for larger organizations.
Management Style	Command and Control	Consensus	If you already have a strong command and control organizational structure, you might be able to take advantage of them to get the job done quickly.
Cultural Tradition	Western (North) American, West (European)	Eastern (especially Japanese)	Japanese companies have traditionally followed an incremental approach to improvement called Kaizen. Western companies have tended toward drastic innovative and sudden changes.
Previous Experience	In some companies the starburst has too often in the past not been followed by lasting results.	The incremental approach may have proven to be too subtle in the past. No one got the message.	

path is for your organization may require some effort, but the time will be well spent. Little benefit accrues in trying to make the practical changes of implementing IPA when changes to the basic nature of your organization also have to occur. Appendix C contains additional organization-specific variables that may have to be considered in developing your IPA implementation objectives, approach, and plan.

LISTEN TO YOUR CUSTOMERS

It is important to establish and maintain a client-focused approach to development of your IPA implementation plan. The recommended approach is to let the problem drive the solution or, in other words, to base your IPA implementation approach, plan, and objectives on performance issues and customer expectations.

The first step is to identify your customers, which may not be a straightforward task. One useful approach is to answer the question, "Who has a stake in this process and its outcome?" To varying degrees, all stakeholders are customers, but three in particular are important to your planning process, as depicted in Exhibit 3-5.

The first is your company's executive management team. Its goals for the company must be factored into your implementation objectives and approach. These goals might be improved competitiveness, increased market share, and reduced losses or increased profitability, but they may also include company reputation and ability to enter new markets. The second is operations, representing individuals who will receive the training and use the performance tools you develop. Their needs are typically clear performance guidelines and effective tools that add value to their production processes, while assuring performance. The third, but certainly not the least, is your company's customers. They set the standards that your company (executive management and operations) must meet in order to acquire and retain their business, including responsiveness to their expectations.

The best and most direct way to gain the necessary understanding of your customer requirements is to ask, listen, and discuss. In this process, it is important not to project your values on their feedback. In certain cases, customer needs and expectations will be clear, explicit, and documented, perhaps in their own mission statements and policies. In others, it may require your active listening skills and substantive discussions to help your customers identify and articulate their underlying needs and expectations.

SET GOALS, OBJECTIVES, AND METRICS

Your IPA implementation plan will identify and define the specific tasks and actions necessary to achieve the goals and objectives for implementing IPA in your organization. Goals break down the

EXHIBIT 3–5. CUSTOMERS IMPORTANT TO THE IPA PLANNING PROCESS

Company's Customers	
Executive Management	Operations Organizations

mission or vision into more manageable specifics. Objectives identify the specific outcomes that, when achieved, will result in the goals having been met. Good objectives are characterized by certain definable attributes, as listed in Exhibit 3-6.

Your company and your customers will determine the specific goals and objectives for your implementation plan. These goals and objectives will define the nature and extent of integration within your performance assurance organizations and their degree of integration within your business and operations management systems.

EXHIBIT 3-6. ATTRIBUTES OF EFFECTIVE OBJECTIVES

- Measurable (Also see Appendix E on metrics).
- Understandable. Each objective has clear meaning and relevance.
- Necessary. Each objective must be appropriate and lead to achievement of the goals that support the mission.
- Sufficient. Objectives must be comprehensive and complete enough to eliminate gaps that could jeopardize attainment of the mission.
- Attainable. If it is not feasible to achieve an objective, you cannot expect to achieve the goal it supports.
- Economically feasible. Objectives must be cost-effective or they will be doomed to failure.

Performance metrics must be identified in conjunction with development of your implementation objectives to ensure there are clear and established mechanisms for measuring the attainment of those objectives. Meaningful measurements may be quite easy or very difficult to define, depending on the process being measured. For example, if a stated goal is the consistent, systematic, and effective management of risks during company procurement processes, your objectives might be:

- Consistent use of a bid/no-bid risk evaluation process in conjunction with procurement activities.
- Development of risk management plans for acceptable risks.
- Rejection of opportunities that present unacceptable risks to the company.

Potential metrics associated with these objectives would include:

1. Percent of total procurements where a documented bid/no-bid evaluation was completed at the correct point in the process. "Correct point in the process" defines where or how you make your measurement of this metric.

2. Percent of total new projects where unacceptable risks were discovered after project startup.

In the first case, measurement is relatively straightforward and direct. Completion of the bid/no-bid risk evaluation during the procurement process generates records that can be tracked relative to the overall process. The risk evaluation was either completed at the right point or it was not, and the higher the percentage that were, the better. This metric could be effectively measured on a near-continuous basis.

The second metric is more problematic, but because it addresses the effectiveness of the evaluation process (i.e., the process achieves the desired outcome of risk avoidance or risk management or it does not), it can be very important. Measurement of this metric requires an ongoing process of project evaluation and reporting that recognizes and responds to change that occurs during the course of the project activity (change management). Change management is an integral element of project management and should happen as a matter of course. However, measurement of this metric will necessitate reviewing change management records and comparing those records with the original risk management plans to determine instances of unreviewed project risks. Based on the overall considerations of potential risks to the company, this metric may be measured less frequently. Appendix E contains additional tips on establishing and using effective metrics.

THE PLAN

The objectives for your IPA implementation project, and, therefore, the bases for development of your project plan, are as follows:

1. Integrate management and execution of regulatory compliance, environmental protection, health and safety, and quality assurance functions through a single top-level organization.

2. Elevate safety, health, and environmental protection to core-value status within your firm.

3. Align those values with your business and project processes.

The specific methods used to accomplish these objectives will be based on your company's characteristics; at a top task level, however, all organizations should experience the following common planning elements:

- Program development.
- Alignment.
- Communications.
- Tools.
- Training.

The objectives of, and keys to, these top tasks are discussed in the following sections. Specific subtasks that may fall within each top task will be determined by the unique characteristics of your organization.

Program Development

Within an IPA organization, individuals responsible for regulatory compliance, environmental protection, human health and safety, and quality assurance coordinate development and execution of performance assurance plans based on shared performance criteria, goals, and priorities. Integrated measurement systems and feedback processes ensure that the desired level of performance is achieved and improvement opportunities are realized. An effective IPA organization also uses consolidated information systems to identify and respond to specific operational activities and to track performance in each of the four areas identified above.

Your plan must address development and documentation of an IPA organization, or organizational element, that provides the desired cross-program integration. Documentation of roles, responsibilities, and procedures must be sufficient to eliminate ambiguity. However, the additional documentation necessary to support an IPA function should be minimal. It is most useful to work with existing documentation to the extent possible and to develop new documentation only where necessary to address integrated functions.

In developing your plan, it is also useful to recognize that integration within an IPA organization will not be achieved as a step change; instead, it requires a process of evolution. Your plan must provide the proper catalysts and opportunities for this process and define key milestones and objectives, but should also be flexible and take into account that much of the actual process will be driven by your organizational and individual personalities. The desired outcome is an organization that facilitates effective integration of policy and strategy, preserves autonomy at the technical professional level, and integrates the implementation of activity-level performance plans.

Alignment

A key objective of the IPA function is to integrate performance assurance measures directly into operating plans and procedures so that everyone involved in an activity contributes to performance assurance. In this way, the traditional barriers between operations and performance assurance (i.e., regulatory compliance, environmental protection, human health and safety, and quality assurance) begin to break down, and the depth of IPA influence over an activity increases. This is discussed further in the sections on tools and training.

A second key objective is alignment of the IPA function with your other business and operations management systems. These other systems may include contracting and sub-contracting, legal, insurance, marketing/sales/business development, and human resources as well as others applicable to your organization. Alignment will increase the span of IPA influence over your entire organization and is a critical step in full integration of IPA with your company's core management systems. The IPA function can also be an effective ally for these systems by identifying needs and opportunities for their implementation during the course of IPA program activities.

Aligning IPA values with your company's management systems and operations processes is necessary to achieve optimum implementation of performance assurance practices. At CH2M Hill, we are a global project delivery company. We have implemented a comprehensive project delivery process that forms the backbone of our client-focused approach to quality management and provides the framework for aligning IPA core values with operations. The following illustrates alignment of IPA core values with the project delivery process:

- Procurement phase:
  - Screen risks–bid/no-bid.
  - Characterize risks–Proposal:
    — PM characterizes risks and performance objectives and builds risk mitigation or performance assurance into project approach and pricing.

— Tools, resources, and support from IPA.

- Chartering/planning/endorsing phase:
  - Project plans/instructions:
    - Incorporate risk management measures.
  - Risk management objectives and criteria:
    - Clearly communicated and understood by project team.

- Execution/managing change phase:
  - Performance assurance procedures and actions.
  - Management of hazards/risk.
  - Recognize/manage change.

The following sections discuss alignment of several common business and operations management systems with IPA.

CONTRACTING AND SUBCONTRACTING. Your company's contracts and subcontracts are critical vehicles for implementation of IPA processes in the product you provide to your clients and that subcontractors provide to you. Your planning objective should be to incorporate IPA objectives and criteria into contracting and subcontracting processes and procedures. This will positively influence your company's standard contract and subcontract forms and language as well as the processes used to screen and select qualified subcontractors.

A close working relationship with the contracting and subcontracting organizations also produces operational benefits through the opportunities they have to influence positive performance. Because their staff are involved in hiring subcontractors and initiating agreements for executing work and providing services, they are in ideal positions to verify that IPA considerations are addressed in the agreements.

LEGAL. Your legal department shares the IPA objective of risk management and can be an important ally in your implementation process. The legal department frequently manages risk management and loss prevention programs; this makes IPA and legal staff natural partners in the process. As with the contracting and subcontracting staff members, a close working relationship with your legal staff and shared objectives for risk management provide cross-program benefits. In addition, because the legal department manages claims against the company, it is an excellent source of lessons learned that can provide valuable input to continuous improvement processes.

INSURANCE. Your company's insurance coverage is an important element of your overall risk management process, providing coverage for residual and unplanned risks. As is the case with contracting and legal department staff, a number of shared objectives and opportunities exist for cross-program benefits between your IPA and insurance programs. It is extremely valuable for IPA staff to act as advocates for insurance program involvement in project planning efforts, based on the fact that the insurance program may have low visibility within operations groups.

BUSINESS DEVELOPMENT, MARKETING, OR SALES. Your business development organizations may seem like strange bedfellows for an IPA organization, but they actually represent a key resource as well as managing an important step in the performance assurance process. Business development staff members are links to your company's customers, and they can provide you with additional insights into customer expectations and policies in the areas of performance assurance. Interface early in your planning process to tap this source of information.

The business development organizations are also important conduits for getting your information back out to the customers. Business development staff must understand the IPA program, the performance policy and objectives, and the performance assurance processes. They can disseminate this information to your customers, obtain customer feedback, and gradually raise your customers' expectations in the area of performance assurance, thereby providing your company with a competitive advantage. The business development organization is an important ally in your efforts to ensure systematic risk management practices during the procurement process.

HUMAN RESOURCES. Performance is ultimately achieved through the actions of your company's employees, your human resources. One of your key objectives is to instill core values that are shared by all staff. This requires effective communication and staff training to ensure cooperation and teamwork. It may also require a change in the organization's culture to achieve employee ownership of performance. Important additional elements in your implementation planning process are establishing and communicating clear performance expectations and accountability. Accountability should include a system of rewards as well as sanctions, so you should involve your human resources staff early in the implementation process.

Communications

The ultimate objective of your communications processes is to instill a firmwide culture built on awareness, understanding, and acceptance of regulatory compliance, environmental protection, human health and safety, and quality assurance as core values. From a project planning perspective, three key tasks are suggested:

1. Work with management at all levels to build and maintain endorsement of the IPA process and initiative.

2. Provide management teams with information tools and resources to provide valuable management leadership during implementation processes.

3. Provide firmwide information that illustrates and reinforces the importance of safety, health, and environmental protection.

The media you use to accomplish these tasks depend on your company's existing communications processes. In this age of technology, they will undoubtedly include e-mail and voicemail, but caution should be exercised to avoid impersonal messages that have a negative effect.

Tools

Your planning objective is development and implementation of tools and resources that facilitate effective integration of performance assurance measures within your operational processes. These tools should address the needs of the following:

- Operations staff responsible for initiating activity-specific performance assurance measures.

- Performance assurance staff responsible for supporting and monitoring operations.

The types of tools you should consider when developing your implementation plan should be based on feedback you receive from your customers, the nature of your company's operations, and your need to support and monitor operations as well as on what you need to implement performance assurance measures. For illustration, the range of tools to be considered during your planning process is depicted in Exhibit 3-7.

Training

Your training objectives are twofold. First, you must instill a firmwide culture built on awareness, understanding, and acceptance of safety, health, and environmental protection core values that will support the implementation of systematic and consistently applied practices within your company's management systems. This training objective is closely tied to communications processes discussed earlier.

The second training objective is to develop and deliver training that provides staff members with the knowledge and skills necessary to implement performance assurance measures during their business and project activities. Accordingly, this training focuses on information needed to implement performance assurance tools and processes developed that are consistent with your implementation plans.

EXHIBIT 3–7. PLANNING PROJECT TOOLS

IPA Support Role	Risk evaluation and planning support and expertise, review of risk evaluations and management plans, tracking process implementation, assessment of performance, and management of lessons learned.				
Tools and Resources to Support Project Performance Assurance Measures	Risk screening processes, checklists, information, and training.	Risk evaluation checklists, information, and training.	Performance assurance information, resources, and training.	Performance assurance forms, checklists, guidance, and training.	Forms, guidance, and training.
Project Performance Assurance Measures	Screen risks at bid/no-bid stage. Evaluate, mitigate, and price for proposal.	Implement safety and risk management through plans and procedures.	Delegate safety and risk management responsibilities and actions to project staff.	Evaluate and measure risk management performance. Conduct independent oversight.	Review assurance performance and lessons learned.
Project Delivery Process:	Produce proposal.	Establish a team charter. Develop workplan.	Endorse the plan.	Execute the project. Manage change.	Close out the project.

RESOURCE-LOADED SCHEDULE

The last step in establishing your plan, and just before implementation, is to develop a schedule of critical implementation activities, resource-loaded with appropriate personnel and materials to accomplish full implementation. At this stage, management must be willing to provide the necessary resources, and its true commitment to the program can be accurately assessed. By identifying initial cost information for resources and tasks at the beginning of a project, you can predict the total cost of individual tasks, resources, phases, and the entire project. Then you record actual costs as tasks are completed, enabling you to manage tasks and resources to bring the project in on time and within budget.

When you assign resources and costs to your tasks, you can then answer cost-related questions at any point in your project, such as:

- How do you define resource costs for this task?
- How do you define resource costs for the project?
- How much will it cost to complete this task?
- What is the total cost for this phase of the project?
- What is the planned project cost?

A sample schedule in which resources associated with each task and subtask are tabulated and rolled up for the entire implementation process is shown in Exhibit 3-8.

An additional benefit to working with a resource-loaded schedule is the ability to adjust resource expenditures through modifications of the project schedule.

EXHIBIT 3–8. SAMPLE RESOURCE-LOADED SCHEDULE

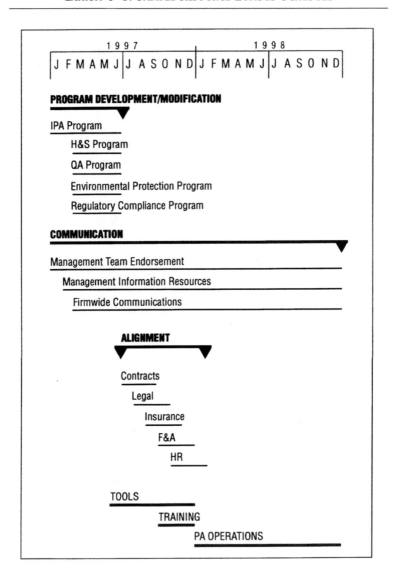

REFERENCES

Dew, John R. (1997). *Quality-Centered Strategic Planning: A Step-by-Step Guide.* New York: Quality Resources.

FOUR

EXECUTION

Chapter 3 explained how to develop the roadmap to successful IPA implementation. This chapter helps you follow your roadmap by providing guidelines for getting off to a good start and installing guideposts along the way to keep you on track.

Integrating risk and requirement management functions positively impacts all business processes. We will discuss CH2M Hill's IPA experience and illustrate how integrating the risk-related functions of regulatory compliance (RC), environmental protection (EP), quality assurance (QA), and health and safety (H&S) can help create a high performance organization that will dominate the future, creating the kind of organization, as described in chapter 1, that is:

- Close to, and driven by, the customer.
- Flexible and agile.
- Able to spontaneously form and re-form high performance project teams.
- Highly integrated and without organizational boundaries.
- Results-oriented.
- Operated by committed employees who truly buy in to the mission and values.

Rather than present extensive case histories, this chapter describes how specific elements were implemented at CH2M Hill and other companies.

At CH2M Hill, the IPA organization was charged with implementing a companywide safety, health, and environmental protection initiative. How IPA and the strategic initiative team interacted is described throughout the chapter.

As a key business management process, IPA provides the means for systematically implementing management responsibilities over an activity life cycle. IPA staff must be involved at the initial goal-setting stage of an activity to ensure that performance elements are included in the planning process. Performance tasking is accomplished when developing written operating procedures that say what we will do. Through effective training and communication, employee ownership is achieved, and we do what we said and record what we did. IPA staff members monitor this process and evaluate the results, leading to performance improvement actions, performer development, and personal and organizational rewards.

LAUNCHING

Once your plan is final, it is time to launch the process. The steps in the process are as follows:

- Develop tools such as databases, checklists, and procedures.

- Establish effective communications with employees (i.e., through education, training, and motivation).

- Conduct a readiness review to determine if you can actually start operating in an integrated way.

DEVELOPING TOOLS

Tools are the aids that help make a process work effectively. They may range from simple forms and checklists that help ensure that certain processes are completed, to complex databases that employ sophisticated data retrieval and even artificial intelligence. The latter might be used, for example, to identify risk elements and mitigation based on job-specific data communicated interactively by using a computer. The tools needed to streamline your IPA process depend on your organization. CH2M Hill's tool development is described in the following section.

Project Delivery Process at CH2M Hill

CH2M Hill is a project delivery company. Although a wide variety of projects are conducted, each with its own risks and requirements, they all have similar attributes. These include the need to deliver quality results to clients on time and within budget. Client satisfaction is vitally important for repeat business and the firm's reputation.

Projects are delivered using a series of steps that, taken together, are called the project delivery process (PDP) (CH2M Hill 1996). They define the chronology of a project, starting with initial business development; they proceed with the proposal; then they are followed by execution, change management, and project closeout. Throughout the process, emphasis is placed on obtaining endorsement or agreement between project team members, clients, and other stakeholders for all aspects of the project.

The PDP provides a consistent framework in which to deliver projects. In itself it does not deal with risk management and requirement identification issues directly. However, the PDP does offer a perfect place to hang tools that do deal with these issues.

In 1997, CH2M Hill embarked on a safety, health, and environmental protection initiative. Within this initiative, tools were developed to help project managers deal with the risks and requirements inherent in their particular projects. These tools were integrated into the PDP so that they would become a normal part of the way all projects are done.

Get the Tools Out There, Then Improve Them

An understandable tendency exists to try to refine tools to perfection before starting to use them. Clearly, diminishing returns set in at some point. While you do not want to subject the organization to an unusable tool, it does not have to be perfect at the start either. Much can be gained by starting with simple tools, then refining them with true improvements over time. This approach has the advantage of starting the operation in a reasonable time as well as allowing the best of all teachers, experience, to work. No amount of planning can take the place of actual job experience to prove out a tool.

Consider starting with a simple, paper-based prototype system before graduating to a sophisticated computer database, for example. The quirks of your process should surface quickly, allowing you to make rapid and cost-effective improvements.

Establishing Effective Communication

Implementing integrated performance assurance means change. Effectively communicating the effect of change on employees is essential. People go through predictable stages when confronted by change. These include awareness, confusion, enthusiasm (or skepticism), learning, effort, doubt, acceptance, and belief (Miller Howard, 1994). You can help by presenting information on the transition as clearly as possible. Include specifics and the desired future state as well as the benefits. A table, as shown in Exhibit 4-1, is a useful way to organize the information in one place.

Exhibit 4–1. Communicating Change

Current State	Transition Actions	Future State	Benefits
Describe specific aspects of the current state.	Enumerate actions that will be required and who will be affected.	Describe this aspect of the future desired state.	List the benefits that accrue from the change.
Next aspect	Present more actions	Another aspect of the future state	More benefits

(Adapted from Miller Howard, 1994)

The Hook

People need a reason or driver to accept the changes inherent in implementing IPA. A hook (i.e., a dramatic incident) to which people can relate is helpful. Within your organization, you may have just the hook you need. The hook is not necessarily a positive or desirable experience. It may even be tragic. For example:

- **An accident.** An accident or credible close call can be an effective hook to convince employees that integrating regulatory compliance, environmental protection, health and safety, and quality assurance is worthwhile. When an accident occurs, investigation frequently reveals that more than health and safety lapses contributed. Very likely degraded quality and environmental compliance issues contributed to the accident as well. A forceful case can easily be made that if the RC, EP, QA, and H&S requirements had all been handled in an integrated system, conditions that led to the accident would have been much less likely to exist. Early in his career, a senior manager of one company lost consciousness and had to be rescued when he entered a confined space with inadequate safety precautions. Recalling the incident years later in discussions with fellow senior managers provided dramatic support for the safety program.

- **A costly mistake.** An example of a costly mistake, or even a credible near-miss, works almost as well as an accident to dramatize the benefits of IPA.

- **Cost analysis.** Simply showing an actual estimate of cost savings achievable through integration provides powerful motivation for those responsible for profitability. The estimate should be realistic and be based on credible conservative assumptions to hit home. Chapter 2 showed one approach to analyzing costs versus benefits of integration.

- **Fear.** Concern over personal safety or legal or regulatory liability can be an effective hook. Showing how IPA implementation can help reduce fear that accidents or other undesired events will occur will provide motivation.

Education, Training, and Motivation

If you want to teach people a new way of thinking,
don't bother trying to teach them.
Instead, give them a tool, the use of which
will lead to new ways of thinking.
— Buckminster Fuller

Information presented well enables learning. When focused and conducted properly, training should change behavior. The results of effective education and training should be knowledge, motivation, and behavior change.

At CH2M Hill, we applied a multifaceted approach to education, training, and motivation. We recognized a need to improve overall employee health and safety awareness as well as to provide specific information about the new systems being put in place.

A safety, health, and environmental protection initiative was implemented. The initiative sought to address corporate culture changes that would result in improved safety awareness for each employee in every action, both at work and at home. In addition, the initiative sought to build safety and risk management processes into all elements of the project delivery process. The job of implementing the processes as well as providing associated education and training was given to the IPA organization.

Training programs and communications outreaches were developed at four levels. To enhance overall safety awareness, an all-hands safety awareness training session was created. To provide information on the safety and risk management processes being integrated into project delivery, communication initiatives (e.g., participation in staff meetings and conference calls) were developed for upper-level line managers, project managers, and functional groups providing performance-affecting support to project delivery. The functional groups included contract administrators and regional health, safety, and quality managers. The information was tailored to meet the needs of each group. Upper-level line managers were given a basic overview and specifics on oversight of the new processes. Project managers were given brief instructions, tools, and checklists to help implement risk management at an operations level. The "give them a tool" approach was much more effective and accepted than a formal training course at the operations level. Performance-impacting functional managers were given information to help them maintain their portion of the risk management processes and understand their personal interactions with each other. In addition, articles were written and distributed in various company publications. All communications outreach activities (training, meetings, and articles) were included as part of a master communications plan, so gaps and overlaps could be identified.

Communications Plan, Media, and Other Details

To effectively manage your communications, especially for a large company, you may find it desirable, even necessary, to write a communications plan. While your communications plan should be crafted to best meet your own needs, including the following topic areas may be helpful:

- **Goals and objectives.** Listing the specific goals and objectives you expect to achieve with individual communication activities helps you define what is needed.

- **Media, mechanisms, and schedule.** Identifying where, when, and how communication activities will occur helps alert you to lead time and interface requirements.

- **Content and audience.** Matching content to audience is probably the most important factor in designing communication activities.

- **Followup.** You have to know if your audience received your message. Approaches to determine this valuable information vary from just asking, to developing performance indicators that will indirectly show the extent to which your audience heard and understood you.

- **Action assignment.** Your plan should identify who is going to do what and when. Otherwise it is very likely that no one will take ownership. This also helps you to see if you are being unrealistic in your demands.

The plan helps identify opportunities, eliminate gaps and overlaps, show areas to emphasize, and generally help track progress. With some analysis (perhaps a survey of recipients), it may be possible to determine which combinations of message, media, and audience work best, allowing optimization of future efforts. Your plan should allow for recording completed communication events as well as showing what is planned. Showing a written record of your communication efforts is valuable for demonstrating results to management.

The optimum communication media depends on your organization's characteristics. Some suggestions follow:

- **Intranet.** Internet technology, more specifically Intranet, a business internal network, may offer one of the best tools to communicate effectively with large numbers of staff. At CH2M Hill, an Intranet site called the "Virtual Office" was developed at the same time as the safety, health, and environmental protection initiative. The Virtual Office provides a platform upon which integrated risk management processes are interwoven into the project delivery process. It is a medium that any employee can access at any time. While effective as an electronic library, it can be even more effective as a project work environment. During project planning, risk-based decision tools such as checklists and forms housed in the Virtual Office are accessible to all and can be completed online by project managers and staff. As the project progresses, integrated project assessments may be conducted with observations recorded online. The user accesses a web page that automatically uploads observations to a database for tracking corrective action and evaluating trends. Because the project is planned online, it generates an easily accessible electronic record from which assessment checklists can easily be generated.

- **E-mail.** E-mail can be a very effective tool for communication if properly targeted and not overused. Avoid "all users" e-mails that tend to clog both the delivery system and individuals' mailboxes. E-mail allows you to tailor your message to your audience by selecting only those individuals who are most likely to be interested in and affected by your message. Different aspects of IPA will be important to different people. In our busy society, everyone wants to know "how will this affect me" first. If time permits, they may be interested further. E-mail permits a dialogue to develop; this tool can be used collectively to answer questions that many have, but perhaps only one asks. Another handy use of e-mail involves posting useful forms and the like on shared e-mail locations. They can then be downloaded as needed. Give some thought to the level of e-mail your recipients get. If they are already overloaded, your message may be contaminated by the receiver's frustration with e-mail in general. You may have to find another medium.

- **Video and teleconferencing.** Video and teleconferencing are rapidly improving in quality and decreasing in price. It is now fairly routine to videoconference training sessions to multiple satellite stations around the world. Many cities have videoconferencing facilities for rent by the hour, decreasing the need for capital investment. Electronic presentations, including interactive, computer-based training modules interspersed with live video, can be transmitted over the Internet, allowing audiences to ask for and receive answers to questions in real time from any location. Audio-only teleconferencing is now routinely used for geographically dispersed staff meetings and many other business interactions.

- **Posters.** They may not be very high-tech, but if you repeatedly see one next to the elevator, you will probably get the message. Posters are most effective if kept simple. You can always give instructions regarding who to contact for more detailed information.

- **Newsletters.** Many organizations have some form of periodic newsletter. It is very likely that the person responsible for newsletter content will be only too happy to place your information in the newsletter. Very frequently, company newsletters go begging for content.

CONDUCTING A READINESS REVIEW

When vision, goals, objectives, metrics, and tools have been developed, it is time to take stock of your readiness to proceed. One excellent approach is an operational readiness review, which is simply a more or less formal determination of whether you have adequately planned your approach. Are there gaps in your plans? If so, now is the time to systematically eliminate them. If all the gaps are covered, are there any places where you have failed to make adequate contingency plans, enabling minor setbacks to derail the whole process? The checklist in Exhibit 4-2 may help to identify holes and weaknesses.

Planning the readiness review consists of identifying required actions. Some examples are included in Exhibit 4-2, but the checklist should be tailored to your needs. A checkmark indicates that completion of this action is required before you can go forward. Initialing and dating over the checkmark provides evidence that the item is complete. For complex or especially involved readiness reviews, it may be helpful to make a second list of exceptions with justifications and contingencies where an action cannot actually be completed before starting IPA implementation. Some items can be deferred if this will not delay startup.

EXHIBIT 4–2. READINESS REVIEW MATRIX

Project No.: _____ Project Title: _____

Readiness Review Action	Activity/Task			
	Preparation and Planning			
Objectives and goals identified, endorsed, and approved				
Roles and responsibilities identified and coordinated				
Training identified, assigned, planned, and budgeted				
Resources (budget, availability, etc.) identified, planned, and coordinated				
Tools identified and planned				
Communication mechanisms planned and coordinated				
Resource-loaded schedule developed, coordinated, and approved				
Implementation plan completed, reviewed, and approved				

Approved by: _____ Date

Project Manager

ASSESSMENT

Soon after launching the IPA process, when it appears to have stabilized, you should begin assessing how it is working. Assessments can take many forms; examples include self- and independent assessment as well as simply reading and interpreting the metrics that measure both IPA and the business as a whole.

It is extremely valuable to use self-monitoring approaches in the application of IPA. Process implementers retain process ownership. When local process ownership is strong, the very act of measuring and recording often leads to improvement by giving staff new ways to look at familiar tasks.

Walk the talk of integration by simultaneously assessing the various portions of IPA. Regulatory controls deal with compliance levels, quality assessments frequently focus on product quality, environmental protection assessments address waste stream quality, and health and safety assessments examine conditions affecting worker health and safety. Integration of these efforts enables more effective staff utilization and allows synergistic process improvements that might otherwise be overlooked. The significant potential for synergy among RC, EP, QA, and H&S is a major advantage of IPA.

TYPES OF ASSESSMENT

Two assessment targets should be considered. We may assess how well the work of the organization is being performed, (i.e., how well projects are being performed or the quality of products), or we may assess how well the IPA process is performing. In either case, both self- and independent assessments can be made. Both assessment approaches have advantages, and a combination is probably more effective than either alone.

Self-Assessment

In this process, the entity performing the work assesses itself. The main advantage is that the work-performing entity knows the most about the work and can make a comprehensive assessment. In addition, the self-assessment cost can be substantially lower than an independent evaluation. The difficulty is that the work-performing entity will not necessarily be completely objective. In fact, the tendency to try to make one's self look good is the primary enemy of effective self-assessment. To counter this problem, an independent organization may develop the assessment checklist and review the results. This approach is not completely foolproof, but if the value of an effective assessment is understood, and negative repercussions associated with the problems discovered are kept to a minimum, self-assessment can be extremely effective.

Independent Assessment

The advantage of an independent assessment is obvious from its name. It is independent and should, therefore, be more objective. One could argue that political considerations may impair objectivity, even during an independent assessment. There are two main disadvantages. The independent assessor most likely will not know the work as well as those performing it and may miss something. Generally, cost constraints demand that independent assessments be conducted quickly; this increases the concern that something important will be missed. Higher cost is the other disadvantage of an independent assessment. The independent assessor is, by definition, not part of the work team. The cost for the assessor to develop an understanding of the work, prior to performing the assessment, may be a significant part of the total cost of the assessment. On the other hand, an independent assessor is frequently a professional who can bring assessment expertise to the activity that those performing the work may not have.

Perhaps the best of both worlds is achieved by combining frequent self-assessments with less frequent independent assessments.

Integrating Assessments

Cost savings can be realized by having one evaluator perform assessments across the RC, EP, QA, and H&S disciplines. While it may be a rare individual with the background to perform assessments in all disciplines at an equivalent level, much can be gained by taking a "red flag" approach. The assessor performs a detailed assessment in a particular skill area, but uses a checklist of red flag items to watch for in other disciplines. The red flag items are developed by those with expertise in the discipline. They must be observable by someone with minimal expertise in the discipline but must act as indices that readily identify areas of concern. When a red flag is tripped, the assessor normally notifies a subject matter expert in the concerned discipline. Another approach involves preplanned responses for the assessor. An example might be to shut down work if a particular safety-threatening red flag is encountered.

USE THE METRICS

Chapter 2 and Appendix E present considerations for developing appropriate metrics to measure the effectiveness of your integrating effort. Now is the time to use them to greatest advantage.

Two basic types of metrics, process and outcome, may be used. Process metrics track how well the process is performing, while outcome metrics measure the final product or outcome of all the processes. Both measures are valuable. Outcome is ultimately most important, but process metrics provide a way to focus on what changes may most effectively improve the outcome.

Careful analysis of all the metric data at your disposal will, in a well-designed system, provide you with the tools you need to determine success and suggest improvements.

REPORTING, TRACKING, AND TRENDING

Your plan should identify frequency and distribution of reports analyzing measurements and assessments. Invest the time to evaluate, summarize, and write recommendations. Management will be more helpful if they fully understand the overall implications. Be prepared to back up the summaries with the background data upon which they are built.

The objective of reporting, tracking, and trending is to quantify performance more or less continuously. Once performance is quantified, it can be compared to industry benchmarks and company goals. Performance tracking helps identify where to focus improvement energy.

COURSE CORRECTIONS: WHAT TO DO WHEN THINGS GO WRONG

Despite your best efforts, integration may go astray. With frequent monitoring of performance measures and midcourse assessments, you should be able to identify problems in time to make corrections.

In one company, integration was rolled out in a phased fashion, with health and safety first, followed by quality assessment, regulatory compliance, and environmental protection. When quality was rolled out, multiple, day-long training sessions were conducted at various offices throughout the company. While some benefit came from these training sessions, it now appears that the benefits did not outweigh the costs. What went wrong? It seems clear that better alignment with other company directions would have made the effort more effective. At the time, a companywide project management process initiative was just beginning. There was only limited interface between the two initiatives. Each could have benefited from a clearer understanding of the common alignment that should exist between them.

It seems clear that there is much to be gained from attaching IPA to already existing company processes. While there may not always be concurrent company initiatives to join, there are always ways to show how IPA contributes to the existing business process alignment. If IPA is seen as an extra activity that employees have to do, rather than a tool to make what they already do work better, it will fail. It will be too difficult for the employee to see the benefits of IPA.

CAPTURING ADDED VALUE

Perhaps the most useful data to evaluate the effectiveness of an IPA function are value-added data. The objective in describing value-added is to measure the positive bottom-line results of applying IPA techniques against the cost. Costs include the combined effect of one-time costs associated with implementing the IPA function and the difference in operating cost for fully integrated performance assurance functions versus the costs of operating independent performance assurance functions. Value includes any direct benefit realized in the form of improved efficiency and decreased reworking as well as the indirect benefit of improved client relations and reputation.

Because IPA is a new way of doing business, the value-added database is not complete. Value-added metrics are still being identified, and the authors look to future applications of IPA to reveal their full range.

COMPUTING ADDED VALUE

In today's competitive world economy, everything an organization does must, in some way, add value. IPA is no exception. Because various programs, including IPA, may compete for value recognition (and funding), it is beneficial to use a consistent method to calculate value-added benefits. One approach is described in the following paragraphs.

Value-added ratio (VAR) is the ratio of total value-added time or cost in a process divided by total process-cycle time or cost (Shannon, 1997). The total value-added time is the time spent doing things that add value for the customer. The total process-cycle time is the time spent doing things that will and will not add value for the customer. The objective is to show that your activity, IPA in this case, increases VAR. Decreasing non-value-added time or cost increases VAR. IPA decreases non-value-added time or cost by decreasing the need to rework (protecting quality) and protecting against the negative consequences of unmanaged risk (liability).

The VAR approach relies on accurately distinguishing between what adds value for the customer and what does not. If that is not obvious, you may have to survey the customer. In general, customer value has two dimensions, perceived importance and performance. Both should be considered when evaluating value-added for the customer. A powerful technique for combining these two important dimensions is importance/performance charting.

The customer is asked to rate specific attributes of your service or product numerically for both importance and performance. The numerical scale is arbitrary, but if you use this approach for comparison, you must be consistent. Attributes to be rated are business-process-specific but might include such

EXHIBIT 4–3. IP CHART

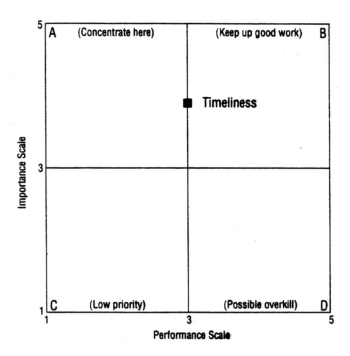

factors as timeliness, accuracy, and completeness. The customer might tell you, for example, that on a scale of 1 to 5 that timeliness rates a 4 in importance and your performance is currently a 3. You could create a metric, call it achieved customer value, to incorporate importance and performance by multiplying the two together. In this case, you have reached an achieved customer value of 12 for timeliness. We will build on this metric later.

At this point, you could graphically portray your status in the customer's eyes by plotting importance versus performance as shown in Exhibit 4-3. This is a common technique called IP charting. By examining the implications of the position of an attribute, timeliness in this case, on the IP chart and considering other business factors, you can begin to make more informed decisions about where improvements should be made in your performance integration effort.

While IP charting is a powerful graphical tool, much can be gained by converting the data to an index that can be analyzed statistically. The potential gain in customer value (PGCV) index is just such a tool (Hom, 1997).

Returning to our timeliness example, our achieved customer value, the product of the customer's importance rating and our current performance rating was 12. That value lacks perspective. We need to know what 12 means relative to what is possible. Generally, unless we can influence customer perception of importance, we only control the performance, so the maximum value that we could expect to achieve for timeliness would be 20 (the importance rating of 4 times the maximum performance rating of 5). Subtracting our achieved customer value of 12 from the ultimate achievable value of 20 tells us where we stand with the customer (12 out of a possible 20). This is defined as the potential gain in customer value (PGCV) index. Comparing the PGCV index for a set of attributes (e.g., timeliness, accuracy, and completeness) focuses attention on the optimum areas for improvement.

The primary reason for advancing from the purely graphical interpretation of the IP chart to the PGCV index is to pack the meaning from the IPA chart into a single number that then can be manipulated statistically. Once the PGCV index is converted to a number, various statistical techniques can be applied to manipulate it (Hom, 1997).

PUBLICIZING YOUR SUCCESS

When identifying and measuring value-added by integrating risk management functions, it is important to remember that you only contribute to improvement of the process that makes the profit, you do not own it. Publicizing success should be subtle. Identify the IPA contribution to the business process in the most quantitative and simple terms. By doing so, you reinforce IPA's role as a vital contributor to the process rather than as an add-on.

In most organizations, opportunities abound to celebrate success and, in particular, your contribution to it. Your communications plan should identify the media, audience, and communication opportunities that will be most effective. Progress updates can be included in the same places (e.g., newsletters, staff meetings, and targeted e-mail) that were used to introduce and train staff in IPA concepts, thus providing closure.

CONTINUOUS IMPROVEMENT

As with any business process, the key to continued success with performance integration lies in taking advantage of every opportunity to improve. Well-designed metrics and periodic assessments are two of the most important tools to facilitate continuous improvement. After initial integration, the improvements will most likely be incremental, causing less stress on other business processes.

Traditional total quality management techniques can be valuable tools to identify and implement continuous improvement as well. Use the techniques you found most helpful during initial integration to facilitate improvement over time. Because each organization is different, and data on successful IPA implementation are not yet abundant, relying on your own empirical integration experience is probably the most direct path to success.

REFERENCES

CH2M Hill and Work Systems Associates. (1996). *Project Delivery— A System and Process for Benchmark Performance.* Denver.

Hom, Willard C. (March 1997). "Make Customer Service Analyses a Little Easier with the PGCV Index." *Quality Progress.* pp. 89–93.

Miller, Lawrence M. et al. (1994). *Whole System Architecture, Beyond Reengineering: Designing the High Performance Organization.* Atlanta: Miller Howard Consulting Group, Inc.

Shannon, Patrick. (March 1997). "The Value-Added Ratio." *Quality Progress.* pp. 94–97.

FIVE

SUMMARY AND CONCLUSIONS

This summary of the salient points that have been presented in the four previous chapters is presented in a form that can be used directly in a compact briefing or sales presentation on IPA. The importance of this type of presentation has been discussed in several of the chapters. A head start on preparing such a presentation may be an advantage for readers.

A common outline for such a briefing is as follows:

- Features.
- Proof.
- Benefits.
- Actions.

Therefore, such will also be the outline of this chapter.

The book allows the reader to understand the fundamentals of the IPA concept, discussed in the introduction, before entering the decision-making phase in chapters 1 and 2 and the planning and implementation phases in chapters 3 and 4. This gives readers the opportunity to decide early if IPA represents good business and is affordable before delving into the details of planning and integration. The extensive use of appendices is our way of offering readers who desire additional, more detailed information our thoughts and communication tools without seriously disrupting the flow of the more general discussions.

The introduction offers some background on both the drivers for IPA and the objectives of its implementation, as well as a working definition. Three main themes are introduced here: the necessity for client focus, the prudence of actively managing risk, and the desirability of integration.

Chapter 1 asks the question, "Is IPA 'good business' in the context of my business environment and goals?" The answers to this question are built on the foundation of well-understood characteristics of successful businesses. To show that the understanding is of more than academic interest, their application in the real world is demonstrated via a CH2M Hill example. The conclusion drawn in this chapter is that for a very wide variety of businesses, the characteristics of the IPA process and the process characteristics of successful business are the same. It is left to the reader to determine if this conclusion is applicable to a specific set of business circumstances.

Chapter 2 asks the question, "Is IPA affordable to implement in my company?" Given that this is a question best answered quantitatively, an optimization approach is offered as a basis. Even though the approach in this chapter applies parameter values in the realistic range, the reader is encouraged to replace those used in the example with real data for the specific business environment being addressed. Straw-man success criteria are also offered to provide the needed transition from data/analysis to information useful in decision making. This is a critical juncture in the book; it is at this point that a reader should be able to make a judgment, with fair confidence, that IPA is a viable option for implementation under a specified set of circumstances.

Chapter 3 begins to lay the groundwork for planning the IPA process, tailored to the business at hand. The constituents of good planning are also constituents of good planning for IPA. The basis of this discussion, therefore, is that any rigorous project management planning process being successfully implemented in a company will also work in planning IPA implementation. In fact, management and employee familiarity with the planning process used to initiate a new program like IPA is a distinct advantage to its successful implementation.

Chapter 4 provides insights into how to get off to a good start in implementing your IPA plan and how to access progress during the early implementation process and beyond. This chapter is supported extensively by appendices that provide the reader with templates and other information that have been used by CH2M Hill in its IPA implementation.

Much remains to be done to fully understand, plan, and implement IPA. The experience base, although impressive, is still meager, and additional performance measures, performance metrics, and performance data are needed to provide tested guidance toward optimizing the utility of IPA. Implementing IPA, while fully understanding that it is a journey, not a destination, in the meantime will enable us all to derive benefits significant to the continued success and growth of our businesses.

Appendix A

IPA VALUE IN BUSINESS SECTORS

This appendix shows how IPA and its elements can apply to a wide variety of different-sized companies with diverse business objectives and settings. Twelve business groups that represent some of CH2M Hill's core clients—both large and small—were selected as examples. The business groups are as follows:

- Chemical/petroleum.
- Environmental management and compliance.
- Environmental restoration.
- Facility operations.
- Industrial waste management.
- Manufacturing, industrials, and technology.
- Risk and ecosystem management.
- Transportation infrastructure.
- Utilities.

- Wastewater collection and treatment.

- Water resources.

- Water treatment and supply.

The following sections outline distinctive characteristics of each business group that suggest the need for an IPA, or an IPA-like, approach to risk management.

The Chemical Industry Group. This group provides process understanding, safety, and pollution prevention; regulatory compliance, automation, instrumentation and control, and ISO 9000 certification; employee safety and community relations; hazards communication, Occupational Safety and Health Administration (OSHA) compliance, strategic environmental planning, management consulting, and design-build-operate services.

Its clients represent the following market segments:

- Commodity chemicals manufacturing.

- Specialty chemicals manufacturing.

- Pharmaceuticals.

- Textiles and fibers.

- Plastics.

- Rubber manufacturing.

The Petroleum Industry. Petroleum industry clients represent the following market segments:

- Exploration and production of crude oil and natural gas.

- Refining crude oil into liquid products including gasoline, diesel fuel, jet fuel, heating oil, and petrochemical feedstocks.

- Transportation of crude oil, natural gas, or refined liquid products through pipelines.

- Marketing petroleum products for wholesale or retail sale.

Although located in the United States, these groups' clients are primarily large multinational companies with global business strategies.

The Environmental Management and Compliance Group. This group provides expertise to assist clients with staff, processes, and tools, enabling them to meet environmental management expectations systematically, while complying with environmental regulations. The main areas of focus include:

- Designing and implementing processes and procedures to accomplish systematic and sound environmental management and compliance.
- Planning facility and corporate operations to accommodate and even thrive under the existing and expected regulatory climate.
- Customizing information services that improve clients' access to information and their ability to make good decisions.
- Auditing and other activities to verify the performance of a client's environmental management and compliance systems.
- Training staff, supervisors, and managers to achieve compliance through routine decisions and operations.
- Assuming the responsibility for meeting regulatory deadlines and maintaining appropriate compliance systems.

Clients belonging to this group include both large and small companies, some with global, others with domestic, operations.

The Environmental Restoration Group. This group focuses on construction aspects of projects. As construction manager at risk or general contractor, the group plans, organizes, and directs remediation of contaminated sites. Construction elements used to deliver these projects include:

- Construction health and safety.
- Construction cost estimating.

- Bidding and proposal procedures.
- Standard construction contracts.
- Procurement and purchasing systems.
- Contractor licenses.
- Insurance and bonding.
- Construction quality assurance/quality control (QA/QC).
- Field construction project controls and management.

Clients of this group include companies of all sizes that have complex remediation needs.

The Facility Operations Group. This group provides technical assistance, training, and startup services in the areas of plant maintenance water or wastewater process control, laboratory, industrial pretreatment, safety, and utility management.

The group focuses on:

- Troubleshooting water and wastewater processes or maintenance problems.
- Filling temporary staffing needs.
- Conducting plant process audits.
- Developing facility-specific standard operating procedures.
- Developing process data management systems.
- Assisting in personnel certification.
- Upgrading maintenance management.

Clients of this group include both large and small municipalities and companies.

The Industrial Waste Management Group. This group seeks solutions to problems with air, water, wastewater, and solid and hazardous wastes. Services of this group include:

- Consulting on characterization of the physical and chemical nature of influent and waste streams, monitoring offsite impacts of air emissions and wastewater discharges, and determining the most effective alternatives available for managing waste streams, both in terms of treatment and disposal reuse.

- Designing selected technologies to treat and control air, water, solid, and hazardous waste streams.

- Providing operations assistance, startup services, and contract operations for clients' air, water, solid, and hazardous waste treatment facilities.

Clients of this group include both large and small companies.

The Manufacturing, Industrial, and Technology Group. This group offers clients the full line of classical services in this area but is also involved in helping clients turn environmental liabilities into corporate assets by employing approaches like insurance cost recovery and air emissions banking. This group serves widely diversified companies that are grouped into several segments:

- Transportation equipment.

- Transportation services.

- Printing, publishing, and allied industries.

- Communications.

- Aerospace for commercial defense and space purposes.

The Risk and Ecosystem Management Group. This group supports clients in regulatory compliance. Strategies for compliance with the National Environmental Policy Act of 1969 (NEPA), the Comprehensive Environmental Response, Compensation, and Liability Act of 1980 (CERCLA), the Resource Conservation and Recovery Act (RCRA), and the Clean Water Act (CWA) are common to this group's clients. Risk-based approaches to site cleanup and remediation issues are proposed to limit liability and provide cost-effective risk reduction approaches. The practice is organized into the following specific areas:

- Habitat management.
- Aquatic biology.
- Treatment wetlands.
- Wetlands mitigation.
- Risk management.

This group serves both large and small clients.

The Transportation Infrastructure Group. This group is represented by the public transit market segment, which aids public agencies and transit operators in determining the feasibility of proposed projects through the planning and environmental processes as well as working toward the project implementation through preliminary and final design. The services provided these clients include:

- Planning and feasibility studies.
- Major investment studies.
- Environmental documentation.
- Permitting studies.
- Special environmental investigations for hazardous materials.
- Assistance with conceptual, preliminary, and final designs.
- Utility work.
- Cost estimating.
- Construction services.

The Utilities Group. This group covers both the environmental and transmission and distribution systems market segments. Four types of businesses make up the client group:

- Electric utilities independent power producers.
- Gas utilities independent power producers.
- Gas transmission companies.
- Telecommunications service companies.

These clients range from very small to very large companies.

The Wastewater Collection and Treatment Group. This group deals with management of municipal wastewater, from collection through disposal, including by-products such as air emissions and treatment residuals. Technology focal points are the analysis, planning design, and optimization of collection, treatment, and disposal systems. The practice is organized into the following specific areas:

- Collection.
- Treatment (general).
- Nutrient removal plant analysis technologies.
- Air quality.
- Odor control.
- Residuals.

This group has an international focus and seeks to achieve strong technical involvement across a wide spectrum of clients.

The Water Resources Group. This group focuses on planning, management, and use of water resources. The practice encompasses challenges ranging from maintaining adequate supplies to meet demands to balancing the needs of the environment with water-system operations. The group focuses on the following areas:

- Watershed management.
- Groundwater resources.
- Aquifer storage and resource recovery.
- Agricultural services.
- River systems engineering.
- Stormwater management.
- Combined sewer/sanitary sewer overflow management.

This group primarily serves both large and small governmental groups.

The Water Treatment and Supply Group. This group contains a stable of technologies associated with providing services for public potable water supply as well as water reuse for potable and nonpotable purposes. The group focuses on the following technologies:

- Conventional water treatment technologies like clarification, softening, and filtration.
- Newer, but established, technologies like ozone, ultraviolet, and membranes.
- Developing technologies like organics separation, synthetic adsorption processes, high-resistance magnetic filtration, and electrochemical ion exchange.

This group serves primarily governmental units responsible for supplying healthy water to the general population.

EXHIBIT A–1. HEALTH AND SAFETY AND ENVIRONMENTAL
APPLICATION CHARACTERISTICS

	Environmental Protection	Health and Safety	Quality Assurance	Regulatory Compliance	Value of Integration
Chemical/Petroleum	4	5	5	5	4
Environmental Management and Compliance	5	5	5	5	4
Environmental Restoration	5	5	5	5	5
Facility Operations	4	5	5	5	5
Industrial Waste Management	5	5	4	5	4
Manufacturing	4	5	5	5	4
Risk and Ecosystem Management	5	3	5	5	4
Transportation Infra-structure	4	4	5	4	3
Utilities	5	5	4	5	4
Wastewater Collection and Treatment	5	4	5	5	4
Water Resources	5	4	5	5	4
Water Treatment and Supply	5	5	5	5	4

1 – Not Applicable
2 – Not Important
3 – Somewhat Important
4 – Important
5 – Very Important

The CH2M Hill program managers for each of these 12 business group practices were asked to rate the importance of the four IPA elements to conducting business and of having a fully implemented IPA process for client projects. The results are shown in Exhibit A-1. More than half of all responses fall into the "very important" category. No discernible correlation was seen between the distribution of responses from program owners of very large to very small business types. Nearly all of the remaining responses fall within the "important" category. The number of "important" and "very important" entries over various types and sizes of businesses illustrates the potential utility of the IPA approach in the minds of the program owners and their clients.

Case History Arguments for IPA

The following case summaries are provided as evidence to support the need for, and the value of, strong performance assurance processes that are well integrated into business and operating management systems. Many more illustrations are to be found in a range of available publications, including the Bureau of National Affairs (BNA) reports, *Constructor*, and *Engineering Report*.

Commonwealth v. Consolidated Smelting and Refining Corp. and Master Metals Industries Inc., Massachusetts Superior Court

Two Massachusetts metal companies and their top executives were indicted in state court on November 14, 1996, on charges of assault and battery against employees for exposing them to lead, cadmium, and dangerous solvents. The case marks the first time the state has used assault and battery charges to prosecute companies for ignoring environmental regulations and jeopardizing workers' health, according to Massachusetts law enforcement and environmental officials.

The indictments accuse Consolidated Smelting and Refining Corp., in Sutton, Massachusetts, and a company official of assault and battery by means of a dangerous weapon on two employees, violating the state's clean air act, and illegally transferring hazardous waste to an unlicensed hauler. Master Metals Industries Inc., also located in Sutton, and one of its officials were charged with assault and battery as well as hazardous waste disposal violations.

The state has been examining these types of cases over the past six years and considers this kind of court action to be a strategy when sufficient evidence is present.

KAISER ALUMINUM & CHEMICAL CORP. VS. CATELLUS DEVELOPMENT CORP.

An excavator who moved contaminated soil during the course of housing project construction operations was deemed an operator of a hazardous waste facility and a transporter of hazardous waste under sections 107(a)(2) and (4) of the Comprehensive Environmental Response Compensation and Liability Act (CERCLA). No materials were removed from the site, and there was no knowledge at the time that contamination was present.

GANTON TECHNOLOGIES VS. QUADION CORP.

An engineering firm and a remediation construction contractor, under contract to Quadion to remediate PCB contamination at an industrial site (Ganton), were deemed subject to CERCLA liabilities as operators. They were therefore responsible for exacerbating site contamination conditions. It was argued that (as engineer and contractor) they did not cause disposal of wastes to occur and had no control over the causes of site contamination. The court, however, ruled that disposal is not limited to the initial introduction of contamination into a site. Moving pre-existing contaminants therefore constitutes new disposal.

TIPPINS INCORPORATED VS. USX CORP.

The contractor was found liable as a transporter of hazardous waste because it contributed to the selection of a disposal facility despite the fact that the owner made disposal decisions. The court concluded that a person is liable as a transporter not only in those cases where the person selects the disposal facility, but also when the individual actively participates in the selection process to the extent that he or she has substantial input to the selection decision. In this case, the contractor identified two qualified disposal facilities and obtained disposal cost information for the customers' use in making the decision.

U.S. DEPARTMENT OF ENERGY (DOE) HANFORD SITE ENVIRONMENTAL HEALTH AND SAFETY (EHS) INTEGRATION

As part of its comprehensive reengineering initiative, the DOE's operations contractor integrated its EHS management systems to streamline the numerous performance assurance activities associated with the site's remediation projects. The positive effects of this integration included reduced costs, improved productivity, shortened schedules, increased accountability, and staff ownership. The integration process also led to developing planning tools for individuals actually involved in the execution of work activities to use to evaluate health and safety hazards and implement appropriate mitigation measures during the operations planning process.

ELECTRIC ENGINE MANUFACTURER

An Italian firm, Maselli Motori S.P.A., in Arzignano (VI), employing 500 people, with annual sales totaling $76,500,000, produces electric engines of all dimensions (Oliva, 1997). They obtained quality system certification (ISO 9001) in 1995. In October 1996, they began implementing the environmental management system (ISO 14001), completing implementation in May 1997.

Two employees worked full time (the heads of the safety and the quality assurance divisions). The head of the quality assurance division oversaw the entire project. These employees were supported by two engineers completing their master's degrees by fulfilling onsite training assignments.

The project involved various business functions (e.g., purchasing and maintenance) concerned with operating procedures impacted by ISO 14001. Project completion was relatively problem-free because the staff bought in to the process. The safety director function was created four to five years before implementing ISO 14001. The most significant change was building an adequate area for storing raw material.

In organizational terms, the main benefits were as follows:

- The staff responded positively to the process.

- The staff now has a datum point for matters pertaining to environmental protection and safety (they already had one for quality assurance).

- The designers and the head of purchases improved machinery and plant facilities.

- Cost benefits were realized.

- Fruitful collaboration developed between the heads of quality assurance and safety. (The quality head's systemic perspective was very useful for the head of safety, who began to structure his work in a more complete and systemic way.)

Some savings cannot currently be quantified (it will take several years to obtain a significant cost/benefit analysis), but it is possible to outline the benefit areas. They are as follows:

- Lower waste treatment costs.

- Lower raw material costs (mainly water for work processes).

- Lower energy costs.

Costs for this project were approximately $70,000, including storage area modifications that slightly exceeded ISO 14001 requriements. They consisted of the following:

- Training courses.

- Technical consultants (i.e., a noise survey and soil analyses).

- Outer storage area modifications.

The ISO 14001 project resulted in real integration between quality and environmental management systems. In fact, an employee under the project leader's management is responsible for centralizing functions sharing procedures and inspection processes.

During ISO 14001 implementation, the need to integrate the safety function became clear (the two department heads already worked together and shared many safety concerns), particularly in terms of coordinating unique functions.

The next project undertaken may be implementation of an occupational health and safety management system consistent with BS 8800 norms. In general, management is persuaded that this process will add value to the firm if it is sold, generally improving its image in terms of safety and profitability. These factors, together, led the firm to adopt ISO 14001, integrating quality assessment and environmental protection. The firm subsequently contemplated integrating health and safety.

ELECTRONICS ENGINEERING

This case concerns an Italian electronics firm, GE Procond Electronica S.P.A., in Longasone (BL), owned by a large American company. The firm employs 360 people and its sales are $56,800,000. It was ISO 9001-certified in 1992. The quality manual was written with a strong environmental commitment (mainly to fulfill legal requirements) both in terms of production processes and the product itself. Therefore, plant organization reflected this commitment to safety and the environment. A project for ISO 14001 certification is currently under way. The quality assurance director will head the project, which will last nine months. It will involve one person full time, one person half time, and four part-time workers.

Savings are anticipated in the following cost areas:

- Energy.

- Indirect materials.

- Waste treatment.

- Packaging.

Project cost is anticipated to be approximately $18,000 to $23,000. The biggest part of this sum (approximately $13,000) will be spent for chemical and technical monitoring and analyses. From an organizational standpoint, no particular problems are anticipated due to the current management system (ISO 9001). People are flexible and open-minded, making project implementation a simple matter. This project is being implemented for the following reasons:

- Customer requests (i.e., an absence of cadmium and lower energy consumption).

- Management sensitivity toward environment, quality, and safety functions (particularly observation of the law).

- Integration between the GE Procond targets and corporate guidelines.

REFERENCES

Oliva, Andrea. (June 1997). Personal correspondence via Internet. Oderzo, Italy.

Appendix C

ORGANIZATION-SPECIFIC VARIABLES TO CONSIDER

Your approach to implementing IPA should be predicated on a thorough understanding of the attributes of your organization that are most likely to affect your success. A force field approach can help you visualize the driving and resisting forces that will be most important in your organization. Because these forces differ from one organization to another, a generic solution is impractical. Instead you must tailor IPA to your unique situation, and the force field tool helps you focus on what is most important to your organization.

Consider the force field analysis diagram shown in Exhibit C-1. First, the existing and future desired states are defined; in this case, the existing state is nonintegrated regulatory compliance, environmental protection, health and safety, and quality assurance functions. The future desired state is fully functioning IPA. Next, driving and resisting forces are brainstormed. The

EXHIBIT C–1. SAMPLE FORCE FIELD DIAGRAM

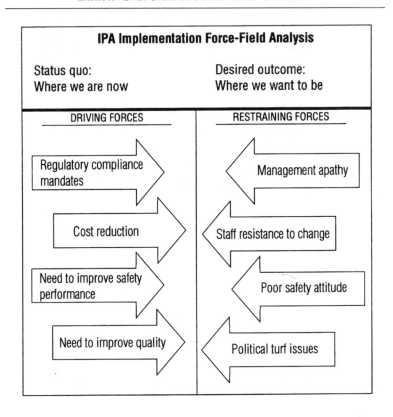

relative magnitude or importance of each force may be graphically portrayed by the size of the arrow. Once all the perceived forces are accounted for, it is time to strategize about how to shift the balance toward the forces that will help achieve the goal (i.e., the driving forces).

Two approaches are possible. The driving forces can be increased, or the resisting forces can be decreased. Because increasing driving force also tends to generate increased resistance, it is usually more efficient to reduce resisting forces, so start with them. Where can the resistance best be reduced and what can be done specifically to bring this about? Resistance forces whose reduction will offer the most rewards should be considered first. After identifying and prioritizing the strategies

EXHIBIT C–2. ORGANIZATIONAL CULTURE SURVEY

No.	Question	Rank
1.	We have a very tall organizational structure and everyone knows exactly where he/she stands in the "pecking order." Everyone knows who is boss.	1 2 3 4 5
2.	Decisions always come down from the top.	1 2 3 4 5
3.	There may be some grumbling, but everyone basically does what they are told.	1 2 3 4 5
4.	"You'll never see anything like a committee or workers group providing input to any decisions around here."	1 2 3 4 5

to reduce resistance, tackle the driving forces. Where can they be bolstered? The final result should be a prioritized punch list of actions that can be expected to unbalance the equilibrium of forces in your favor and result in movement toward the goal of IPA implementation.

WHAT IS YOUR ORGANIZATION'S CULTURE?

TOP-DOWN MANAGEMENT VERSUS CONSENSUS

Can you accurately evaluate your organization's culture? Think about how decisions get made. Does the boss speak and everyone reacts? Or does everyone have to agree before anything can happen? Those extremes define the boundaries of organizational cultures. Your organization probably falls in between. The impact of this on implementing an IPA structure is simply that it will make your life easier and improve your chances of success if you can make the organization's culture work for you instead of against you. This appendix suggests how to get the job done in the two extreme cultures, and you can adapt alternatives to your situation. Exhibit C-2 is a quick test to help evaluate where you are on the organizational culture spectrum. For each of the questions in the exhibit, circle the number that best describes your company, where 1 = strongly disagree (does not fit my organization at all), and 5 = strongly agree (describes my organization extremely well).

Add up your score. The maximum score possible is 20. If you are near the maximum, you have a very top-down organization, with little employee input into decisions. If your score is near the minimum, 4, you have a very consensus-oriented organization. Most organizations fall somewhere in the middle. In some cases, there is consensus management, but only by a few people at the top, with little or no input from the rank and file. Keep your evaluation of your company culture in mind as you work through the rest of this appendix.

Large versus Small Organizations

While you can apply IPA to any size organization, your approach will vary if your organization has many hundreds of employees, compared with a business that can have an "all hands" meeting in your living room. For large organizations, geographic dispersion can present a real challenge. Three areas differ significantly for large and small companies: communications, available overhead funds, and product diversity. These areas are discussed in the following paragraphs.

Communications

At a small company, it may be quite adequate to communicate personally with all the employees. At a large company, whose employees are widely dispersed, communications may become a major issue. CH2M Hill is a company of more than 5,000 employees spread worldwide. Communicating IPA concepts continues to be a complex process.

Available Overhead Funding

Overhead funding to integrate the performance assurance functions in a small company may be practically nonexistent. In a larger company, while overhead may still represent only a small fraction of revenue, its absolute magnitude may be much greater. Thus, the flexibility to spend overhead dollars on setting up an effective IPA process may be much greater in a large organization than a small one. On the other hand, the consolidation of functions represented by IPA makes even more sense for a small company than a large one. When funding will not support a full-time IPA staff, the job can sometimes be an extra duty for existing staff, possibly with technical support from a consultant.

Product or Operational Diversity

Diversity of the organization's business lines may also be a factor in the way you undertake IPA implementation, perhaps indirectly linked to size. Large organizations are likely to have more diverse operations, which demand a broader base of performance assurance functions. CH2M Hill, for example, produces a wide variety of consulting services, which require a broad range of IPA support. Smaller organizations might be expected to be more focused on a limited scope of products and services. Thus, the diversity effect may tend to compensate for the differences between large and small organizations.

DOWNSIZING IMPACTS

Another challenge you may face is lack of available technical expertise. Along with the downsizing/reengineering phenomenon has come the challenge of a dwindling base of technical expertise. If your organization has downsized all or most of your discipline experts in health and safety, quality assurance, regulatory compliance, or environmental protection, you may have a difficult time finding anyone sufficiently qualified to implement an IPA approach. While this may seem like an insurmountable problem at first, IPA may actually provide the long-term path needed to solve some of the problems created by excessive downsizing.

Once implemented, IPA should actually require fewer staff members to operate than the traditional stovepiped multidiscipline approach. However, the approach relies heavily on the ability of each IPA staff member to wear multiple hats. While it is generally unrealistic to expect each person to be fully proficient in all disciplines, the skillful use of tools and processes makes it possible to take the "red flag" approach. The trick is recognizing problems from other disciplines and knowing when to call for help. For example, an IPA staff person with a predominantly quality control background and only passing acquaintance with health and safety tools (e.g., checklists) requires training to recognize potential risk in the health and safety arena. This individual has to be sufficiently in touch with personal limitations to know when to call for expert help. When this approach is well implemented, cost savings result simply because the few experts still available tend to spend their time where their expertise is most valuable.

What if you are so light on discipline-specific technical expertise that there is no one to fall back on? That is the time to consider retaining a consultant or hiring flex staff. Flex staffing or project-specific hiring is becoming more common. With flex or project staffing, employees are hired only for the duration of specific work activities. When the job is over, they are off the payroll. Depending on supply and demand, they may require higher salaries to compensate for lack of long-term commitment on the part of the employer. It may well be worth the extra cost in the short term to get your program started if you can then scale back to core staff for the long term.

While temporary use of outside help may be the only practical way to implement an IPA approach when in-house expertise is inadequate, keep in mind the efficiencies of IPA, which may enable you to drop or decrease the outside help, once you are operating in steady state.

FOR PROFIT VERSUS NONPROFIT

Does it make any difference if my organization is a for-profit company or a nonprofit (e.g., government agency or charity) organization? Really, the big difference is in the metrics that you might use to measure integration. In the for-profit world, lots of profit-oriented financial metrics are already out there, ready to help measure your success in terms that managers understand.

On the other hand, nonprofit organizations may have more of a challenge finding or creating adequate metrics to show the value of IPA implementation to the organization. Some metrics will apply equally well to profit and nonprofit operations. Health and safety statistics are a good example. Accident and injury rates do not depend on whether an organization is for profit. Improved rates, especially if accompanied by decreased health and safety staffing, could be interpreted as an indication of the value of IPA.

Integrating the ISO 9000 and 14000 Families of Standards With IPA

ISO 9000 and 14000 are both now realities. Whether that is important to you depends on your business and where you think the future will lead. Both standards play an increasing role, particularly in international and federal work. More and more requests for proposals (RFPs) require either full certification, or at least programs that meet the requirements of the standards.

A similar management standard for occupational safety and health has met with considerable American industry resistance to date (Zuckerman, 1997). Still, the fact that the controversy exists should lead the prudent manager to seriously consider the possibility of an international health and safety standard on the horizon.

From the beginning of ISO 14000, there has been strong interest in taking advantage of the overlap with ISO 9000, specifically, integrating implementation of the two standards. If an occupational health and safety standard does come to pass, there will undoubtedly be interest in integrating it with ISO 9000 and 14000. The similarities in all management standards beg to be integrated within the implementing organization, if not within the standard-setting process itself.

IPA does not require use of a particular standard for any of its components. Use of ISO 9000 and 14000 as frameworks for two legs of IPA in your organization makes perfect sense, since they were purposely written with many of the same basic requirements. If and when an ISO health and safety standard hits the street, you can be pretty sure that it will also have similar management requirements and that it will make sense to integrate them within your organization. Researchers at the University of Michigan, under the direction of the American Industrial Hygiene Association, have already proposed an occupational health and safety management system that harmonizes with ISO 9000 (Levine and Dyjac, 1997).

The bottom line is that the ideal time to make your organization ISO-compatible or certified would be while you are converting to an IPA organization. The resulting savings could be substantial, both in getting set up, and for the long haul. You could be way ahead of the crowd when three integrated ISO standards become a reality. You get the benefits of integration for your organization as well as the competitive edge of being ahead of the pack.

If you are having trouble getting funding or approval to implement IPA in your organization, you may be able to use the drive for ISO qualification for certification to your advantage. The source of your approval or funding (e.g., the CEO, CFO, or Board of Directors) may not see a clear path to fund IPA but can be convinced of the business necessity of becoming ISO 9000/14000-qualified or certified. A successful tactic in this case might be to push the ISO, then build your ISO system on the IPA model. The ISO registration effort will not suffer; in fact, you will save money by integrating quality and environmental management activities. IPA will come along for a free ride.

REFERENCES

Levine, Steven P., and David T. Dyjack. (April 1997). "Critical Features of an Auditable Management System for an ISO 9000-Compatible Occupational Health and Safety Standard." *AIHA Journal,* 58. pp. 291–297.

Zuckerman, Amy. (March 1997). "Uncertain Future for Management System Standards." *Quality Progress.* pp. 21–23.

Appendix E

CREATING
PERFORMANCE
METRICS

A performance measure consists of a number and a unit of measure. The number tells us how much, and the unit tells us what is being measured. Performance measures must always be tied to a goal or objective. They can be single-dimension units (e.g., hours, meters, or dollars) and show the variation in a process or deviation from design specifications. Single-dimension units of measure usually represent very basic and fundamental assessments of a process or product (DOE, 1995).

More often, multidimensional units of measure are used. These are performance measures expressed as ratios of two or more fundamental units (e.g., miles per gallon or number of accidents per million hours worked). Performance measures expressed this way almost always convey more information than single-dimension or single-unit performance measures.

111

EXHIBIT E–1. TYPICAL METRICS (DOE, 1995)

Measures of...	Measures...	Expressed as ratio of...
Efficiency	Ability of an organization to perform a task.	Actual input/planned input
Effectiveness	Ability of an organization to plan for output from its processes.	Actual output/planned output
Quality	Whether a unit of work was done correctly. Criteria to define "corrrectness" are established by the customers.	Number of units produced correctly/total number of units produced
Timeliness	Whether a unit of work was done on time. Criteria to define "on time" are established by the customers.	Number of units produced on time/total number of units produced
Productivity	The amount of a resource used to produce a unit of work.	Outputs/inputs

Ideally, performance measures should be expressed in the units of measure that are the most meaningful for those who must use or make decisions based on them (DOE, 1995).

For complex systems, many performance metrics may be needed. Information overload can become a problem. Indexing is one answer. An index combines several metrics into a single number. Creating an index can be as simple as computing an average, but more frequently, it is helpful to build a more meaningful index by weighting or applying some more sophisticated algorithm.

Performance measurement is primarily managing outcome, and one of its main purposes is to reduce or eliminate overall variation in the work product or process. The goal is to arrive at sound decisions about actions affecting the product or process and its output. Some typical types of measures are shown in Exhibit E-1 (DOE, 1995).

THE NEED FOR EFFECTIVE METRICS

Effective metrics will achieve the following:

- Identify whether we are meeting customer requirements. How do we know that we are providing the services or products that our customers require?

- Help us understand our processes. Enable us to confirm what we know or reveal what we do not know. Do we know where the problems are?

- Ensure that decisions are based on fact, not on emotion. Are our decisions based upon well-documented facts and figures or on intuition and gut feelings?

- Show where improvements have to be made. Where can we do better? How can we improve our performance?

- Show if improvements actually happened. Do we have a clear picture?

- Reveal problems that bias, emotion, and longevity cover up. If we have been doing our jobs for a long time without measurements, we might incorrectly assume that things are going well. (They may or may not be, but without measurements there is no way to tell.)

- Identify whether suppliers are meeting our requirements. Do our suppliers know if our requirements are being met?

- Allow us to manage and control activities. If you cannot measure an activity, you cannot control it. If you cannot control it, you cannot manage it. Without dependable measurements, intelligent decisions cannot be made.

- Act as guidelines for control, self- and management assessment, and continuous improvement.

CHARACTERISTICS OF EFFECTIVE METRICS

Most performance measures can be grouped into one of the following general categories:

- Effectiveness—conformance to requirements. (Are we doing the right things?)

- Efficiency—desired result at minimum cost. (Are we doing things right?)

- Quality—meeting customer requirements and expectations.

- Timeliness—work done correctly and on time.

- Productivity—value-added divided by cost.

- Safety—measures the overall health of the organization and the working environment of employees.

Metrics must be based on goals and objectives and fulfill the following goals:

- Reflect the customer's needs as well as our own.

- Provide an agreed-upon basis for decision making.

- Be understandable.

- Be broadly applicable.

- Be uniformly interpreted.

- Be measurable.

- Be precise.

- Be economical.

The DOE provides the following observations regarding metrics (it may be helpful to review these before beginning the steps to creating useful metrics):

- The more direct the better.

- Define exactly how to collect the data for the indicator and how to make the computation. Then make sure everyone understands.

- If you cannot flow-chart the process you want to improve, a performance measure will offer little insight into what actions you should take.

- Use the numbers to help people improve, not to judge people.

- Learn to understand variation. You will be more effective.

- Only management can improve a controlled process.

- Ignorance of variation is not bliss. It increases variation.

- We insist on driver's education for those who want to drive; we should insist on statistical education for those who want to set goals for others.

- We learn when a curious person sees an unusual event and acts.

- Once you collect the data, you have to analyze your situation sufficiently, determine if you are in or out of control, then take action.

STEP-BY-STEP METRIC DEVELOPMENT

While different organizations will certainly develop different metrics to quantify IPA implementation efforts, a common six-step process provides an effective framework for most metric development (adapted from DOE, 1995).

1. **Identify the process you want to measure.** You should be able to flow-chart your process. If you cannot, beware! You probably lack a process, and what you do have probably cannot be measured successfully.

2. **Identify critical activities to be measured.** The key question here is, "What do we want to know?" It is disturbingly easy to latch on to measuring an activity because it is relatively easy to measure, when in reality, it is not even a critical activity.

3. **Establish goals or standards.** This provides the basis for comparison. In some cases (such as in certain health and

safety areas), standards are already there, and the process of setting goals becomes much easier. This is also where benchmarking may provide useful goals. In a competitive environment, meeting or beating the benchmarks of the competition may be the goal.

4. **Establish performance measures.** This is a multistep process in which what you want to know is translated into a measurable entity. First, the raw data to be collected must be identified. The metric will likely be derived from, but not actually be, the raw data. The algorithm that converts the data to the metric must be known or designed. The sensor that will collect the data must be selected with consideration of its ability to produce sufficiently accurate, precise, and stable data for the purpose. Sensors may be humans, mechanisms, or a combination thereof. Who will collect the data must be determined; then the frequency of data collection must be established.

5. **Collect data, analyze, and report results.** Once data are collected, analyzed, and reported, you can act on the results. It is important to present the data in such a way that appropriate decisions can be made on the basis of the observation. This will likely involve interpreting and rendering judgment on the significance of the results relative to goals, benchmarks, and standards.

6. **Implement corrective action.** Implementing corrective action closes the loop.

The following factors should be considered when reporting performance measures (DOE, 1995):

- Who is the audience?

- What is the intended use of the data? Will they be used to support decisions and take actions, or will they just be used to monitor performance?

- What is the basic message you want to communicate? (We are here, and this is how we are doing.)

- What is the presentation format (e.g., report, brochure, or oral presentation)?

- What is the underlying nature of the data and any assumptions?

- Is there a trend over time?

- Should I take any action? What kind of action should I take?

- What contributes the most to the total? (It is often most effective to focus on the vital few.)

- Are we focusing on the highest priority actions?

REFERENCES

U.S. Department of Energy. (October 1995). *A Handbook of Techniques and Tools*. Training Resources and Data Exchange (TRADE). Oak Ridge Institute for Science and Education.

Appendix F

COMPANY SURVEY

About 40 small, large, national, or international organizations in Holland, Italy, Australia, Norway, and the United States were contacted directly by telephone or through the Internet to obtain information about integration of their performance assurance programs. Additional information was accumulated through conversations, or from material published on the Internet by firms, associations, and standard-setting organizations. The companies are listed in Exhibit F-1.

Less than half of the companies that were contacted responded. The majority of respondents indicated that they did not have IPA. A few small consulting or nonmanufacturing firms responded that they did not have the appropriate business activities for IPA. Several companies have integrated quality assurance, safety, or environmental compliance with their production functions. The survey did not reveal the extent to which the U.S. government has integrated quality assurance, safety and health, regulatory compliance, or environmental protection, but the Department of Energy and the U.S. Air Force have published extensively on development and use of performance metrics, a critical component of IPA.

Four major companies with from one to more than ten years of integration experience with some IPA elements were contacted, but they did not provide details on their experiences. A major manufacturer of commercial airplanes has only recently begun an integration program and has not yet acquired sufficient hard data about its IPA experiences. However, the company is an enthusiastic proponent of integration and sees it as a natural result of the company's vision and maturity level. Although details are unavailable, one company appeared to have had an "emotional event" that precipitated increased implementation of quality assurance which, in turn, led to IPA.

Respondents from smaller businesses indicate that they are unofficially integrated. One person may have several responsibilities and, perforce, make integrated decisions. However, depending on the individual, this can be an ineffective integration, especially when manuals and other documentation exist for the separate IPA elements.

A U.S. safety/management consulting firm indicated that integration is a promising and expanding business for them, but they have no substantial accumulation of cases yet. Some European businesses appear to have a real, ongoing need for integration. The Scandinavian countries, The Netherlands, and Italy all have consulting groups providing integration products and services to clients. An Australian consulting firm and a water utility also indicate that integration is now a part of their businesses.

EXHIBIT F–1. ORGANIZATIONS CONTACTED ABOUT IPA

ADAC Laboratories – Milpitas CA

Air Cargo Management Group – Seattle WA

Alcoa - Davenport IA

Alcoa/NW Alloys – Spokane WA

Allied Signal – Phoenix AZ

Ames Rubber Corporation – Hamburg NJ

BHP – Broken Hill, Australia

Boeing Commercial Airplane Group – Seattle WA

Department of Energy

DuPont – Spruance Plant, Richmond VA

Energy Laboratories – Casper WY

Fluke Instruments – Everett WA

Fred Hutchinson Cancer Research Center – Seattle WA

Freeshop Online – Seattle WA

Greg Hutchins – US consulting firm – Portland OR

GTW - US consulting firm – Federal Way WA

Intel Corp. – Portland OR/ DuPont WA

Sistemi Gestionali Ecocompatibili – Italian consulting firm

Mountain Safety Research – Seattle WA

Oberto Sausage Co. – Kent WA

Physio-Control – Redmond WA

Providence Hospital – Seattle WA

Radian Corporation – Austin TX

REI, Inc. – Auburn WA

SouthEast Water Utility – Melbourne, Australia

Starbucks – Seattle WA

Summersun Greenhouse Co. – Mt. Vernon WA

Tektronix – Portland OR

The Sapphire Group, Inc. – Washington DC

TNO/Bouw – Dutch consulting firm

Triangel AS – Norwegian consulting firm

Trident Precision Manufacturing – Webster NY

US Air Force (training group)

Warner-Lambert – NJ

Weyerhaeuser – Federal Way WA

Wizards of the Coast – Seattle WA

Zymogenetics – Seattle WA

Appendix G

IPA PRESENTATIONS TO MANAGEMENT

During implementation, you may have to present the essentials of IPA to different levels of management. Exhibit G-1 is a sample presentation for highest level corporate management adapted from CH2M Hill. Exhibit G-2 is a similar presentation for operations level management.

EXHIBIT G–1. PRESENTATION TO CORPORATE MANAGEMENT

Integrated Performance Assurance

Integrated Approach to Safety, Health, and Environmental Protection

CH2M HILL

CH2M HILL   10/10/97   1

Broad Issues

- Risks on Construction Projects
- Effective Safety and Risk Management
  - Subcontractor Safety
  - Contract Compliance
  - Insurance
- Company Marketability

CH2M HILL   10/10/97   2

Definitions

■ Assurance
  - Systematic and Verifiable Processes and Approach to Performance

CH2M HILL   10/10/97   3

Definitions

■ Risk
  - Exposure to a Negative Consequence
    ■ Safety and Health
    ■ Environmental Protection/Regulatory Compliance
    ■ Contractual/Legal
    ■ Technology/Performance

CH2M HILL   10/10/97   4

EXHIBIT G–1. PRESENTATION TO CORPORATE MANAGEMENT (CONT.)

Significance

■ **Performance Is the Basis for Our Customers:**
- Selection
- Payment
- Penalties

CH2M HILL   10/10/97   5

Significance

■ **Job Is Getting Tougher**
- Customer Demands
- New Project Roles
- Competition Is Fierce
- Greater Demands Placed on PM

CH2M HILL   10/10/97   6

Price of Failure
Is Getting Higher

- Larger Stake in Fewer Contracts
- Opportunities for Failure Have Increased
- Clients Tracking and Reporting Performance

CH2M HILL   10/10/97   7

Safety Net Is Necessary

- Systematic Practices
- Integrated into Our Business and Project Processes
  - Support System for Operations
  - Verification for Operations Managers

CH2M HILL   10/10/97   8

EXHIBIT G–1. PRESENTATION TO CORPORATE MANAGEMENT (CONT.)

Operational Concept

■ Integrate Risk Management Within the Operations Process
  – Enhance Our Existing Project Delivery Processes vs. Adding or Replacing Processes

CH2M HILL   10/10/97   9

Process Integration

■ Procurement Phase
■ Chartering/Planning/Endorsing Phase
■ Execution/Managing Change Phase

CH2M HILL   10/10/97   10

Procurement Phase

- Screen Risks - Bid/No-Bid
- Characterize Risks - Proposal
  - PM Characterizes Risks and Performance Objectives, Builds Risk Mitigation/ Performance Assurance into Project Approach and Pricing
  - Tools, Resources, Support from IPA

CH2M HILL   10/10/97   11

Chartering/Planning/ Endorsing Phase

- Project Plans/Instructions
  - Incorporate Risk Management Measures
- Risk Management Objectives and Criteria
  - Clearly Communicated and Understood by Project Team

CH2M HILL   10/10/97   12

Execution/Managing Phase Change

- Procedures and Actions
- Manage Hazards/Risk
- Recognize/Manage Change

CH2M HILL   10/10/97   13

All Phases

- Independent Oversight, Verification, Coordination
  - Status, Summary Information, Results, and Feedback
- Technical Support/Resources
  - IPA (Regulatory Compliance, Environmental Protection, Health and Safety, and Quality Assurance)

CH2M HILL   10/10/97   14

Action

■ **IPA Initiative Under Development**
  – Work With Operations Staff
  – Develop Performance Resources, Information and Systematic Practices
  – Integrate Into Project Delivery Process

CH2M HILL   10/10/97   15

Action Elements

■ **Program Development**
■ **Communications**
■ **Alignment**
  – Operations Processes
  – Other Performance Programs
■ **Develop Tools**
■ **Conduct Training**

CH2M HILL   10/10/97   16

EXHIBIT G–1. PRESENTATION TO CORPORATE MANAGEMENT (CONT.)

Immediate Actions

■ Use Existing Local Resources
- – Operations Manager
- – Contract Administrator
- – Health and Safety Manager
- – Quality Manager
- – Environmental Compliance Staff

CH2M HILL   10/10/97   17

Exhibit G–2. Presentation to Operations Management

Integrated Performance Assurance

CH2M HILL

Definitions

- Performance
  - Doing <u>All</u> the Right Things, and Doing Them Correctly

EXHIBIT G–2. PRESENTATION TO OPERATIONS MANAGEMENT (CONT.)

Market Significance

- Safety Is Our Customer's Expectation
- <u>Safety</u> Is a Competitive Advantage
- Safety <u>Pays</u> and Drives Quality

CH2M HILL   10/10/97   3

Internal Perspective

- Firm Is at Risk
    - Safety and Health
    - Environmental Protection/Regulatory Compliance
    - Contractual/Legal/Insurance
    - Technology/Performance

CH2M HILL   10/10/97   4

Internal Perspective

■ Risks Are Increasing
  – Organizations Are Changing
  – Taking on New Project Roles
  – New/Iincreased Demands on Projects and
    PMs

CH2M HILL   10/10/97   5

Price of Failure

■ IMPACTS OUR PEOPLE
■ IMPACTS TOP AND BOTTOM LINE
  – Loss of Market Share and Opportunities
  – Increased Insurance Cost
  – Direct Costs

CH2M HILL   10/10/97   6

EXHIBIT G–2. PRESENTATION TO OPERATIONS MANAGEMENT (CONT.)

Recommended Solution

- Elevate Safety and Risk Management to Core Value Status
- Top-Down Into Projects

CH2M HILL   10/10/97   7

Desired Outcome

- Systematic Practices and Behaviors
- Integral to Our Business and Project Processes
- Value Added to Clients, Firm, Staff, and Projects

CH2M HILL   10/10/97   8

Exhibit G–2. Presentation to Operations Management (Cont.)

Benchmarks

- OSHA - Voluntary Protection Program (VPP)
- CMA - Responsible Care
- Safety Is Behavior-Based, Not Compliance With Standards

CH2M HILL   10/10/97   9

Concept Application

- Management Leadership
- Staff Training
- Project Analysis
- Safety/Risk Mitigation and Control

CH2M HILL   10/10/97   10

EXHIBIT G–2. PRESENTATION TO OPERATIONS MANAGEMENT (CONT.)

Management Leadership

- Policy/Commitment
- Implementation and Resources
- Followup
- Consequences

CH2M HILL   10/10/97   11

Staff Training

- Policy
- Criteria and Objectives
- Responsibility and Accountability
- Procedures and Practices
- Resources

CH2M HILL   10/10/97   12

Project Analysis

- Project Manager Responsibility
- Resources/Expertise
  - Contracts Administrators (KA), Legal, Insurance
  - Health and Safety
  - Regulatory Compliance
- Risk Evaluation
  - Bid/No-Bid
  - Project Planning Criteria

CH2M HILL   10/10/97   13

Mitigation and Control

- Safety and Risk Management Plans/Procedures
  - Checklists
  - Review and Approval Processes
  - Status Reporting Required

CH2M HILL   10/10/97   14

EXHIBIT G–2. PRESENTATION TO OPERATIONS MANAGEMENT (CONT.)

Challenge

■ Making It Work
 – Positive Activity Control Before Startup
 – Compliance With Defined Processes
 – Accountability

CH2M HILL   10/10/97   15

Action

■ Executive Leadership Team
 – Endorsement and Direction to Proceed
■ Integrated Performance Assurance
 Program
 – Convene Action Team
 – Detailed Action Plan
 – Implement

CH2M HILL   10/10/97   16

Appendix H

SAMPLE TRAINING PRESENTATIONS

Staff will need training in their roles, both during and after IPA implementation. The attached exhibits are adapted from day-long training sessions CH2M Hill presented to various functional groups. This training was specifically oriented toward phasing in quality assurance functions but also presented the elements of IPA.

EXHIBIT H–1. WORKSHOP 1

PM and Onsite Performance Assurance Specialist (OPAS) Quality Workshop

CH2M HILL

Acronyms Used in This Presentation

- PM - Project Manager
- OPAS - Onsite Performance Assurance Specialist
- PAM - Performance Assurance Manager
- D&CAR - Deficiency and Corrective Action Report
- QMP - Quality Management Plan
- SOW - Statement of Work
- PQP - Project Quality Plan
- SSC - Site Safety Coordinator

EXHIBIT H–1. WORKSHOP 1 (CONT.)

Objective and Scope

- Familiarize You With:
  - Quality Management Program
  - Integrated Performance Assurance (IPA) Organization
  - Project Manager (PM)/Performance Assurance Manager (PAM)/OPAS Responsibilities

Videotaped Message From the President

- Top Management Support Is Essential
- Quality Is Everyone's Responsibility
- Quality Effort Must Add Value
- Quality Management Will Help Reduce Risk

EXHIBIT H–1. WORKSHOP 1 (CONT.)

Capsule and Contents

■ Why IPA?

■ What Is Basis of Quality Program?

■ How Will We Implement?

■ PM/PAM/OPAS Roles and Responsibilities

Why Integrated Performance Assurance?

■ Similar Support Functions (Health and Safety [H&S], Quality, Compliance)

■ Reduce Risk

■ Add Value (CH2M HILL Examples)

■ Meet Contract Requirements

■ Meet Recognized Standards

EXHIBIT H–1. WORKSHOP 1 (CONT.)

What Is the Basis of the Quality Program?

■ Risk Management
■ Graded Approach

How Will We Implement the Program?

■ IPA Organization
■ PAM/OPAS Roles and Responsibilities
■ Quality Resources
  • QMP
  • Checklists
  • Staff (PAM, OPAS, Quality Director)
■ Teamwork

EXHIBIT H–1. WORKSHOP 1 (CONT.)

PM Roles and Responsibilities

- Overall Responsibility for Assigned Projects
- Planning (Project Quality Plan [PQP])

PAM Roles and Responsibilities

- PM Interface
- Project Quality Planning
- Procurement Interface
- Coordinating OPAS Activities
- Assessment/Audit/Deficiency Reporting (D&CAR)
- Conflict Resolution
- Tracking/Trending
- Reporting

EXHIBIT H–1. WORKSHOP 1 (CONT.)

OPAS Roles and Responsibilities

- Field Surveillance
- Procurement Interface
- Conflict Resolution
- Assistance to PM (Graded Approach)
- Site Safety Coordinator (SSC)
- Deficiency Identification/Correction
- Reporting

Conflict Resolution

- Sample Scenarios
- Boundaries/Responsibilities
- Teamwork/Communication
- Resources/Safety Net

EXHIBIT H–1. WORKSHOP 1 (CONT.)

Sample Project Planning Walkthrough

- Navigating the Quality Management Plan
- Develop Statement of Work Activity List
- Develop Project Quality Plan (PQP)
  - Apply Risk-Based, Graded Approach
- Quality Cost Estimate Spreadsheet
- Benefit Analysis (Tangible and Intangible Value Added)

PQP to Quality Cost Estimate Decision Diagram

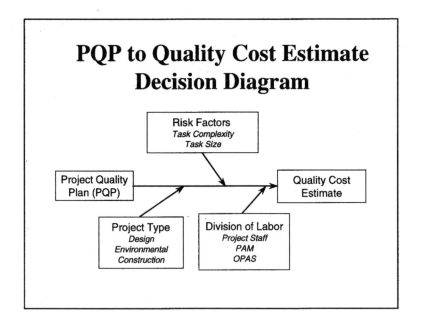

Explanation of Workshop Assignment

- Split into Groups
- PQP (1 Activity/Group)
- Group Presentations
  - Present/Justify Graded Approach
- Class Participation Quality Cost Estimate
- Benefit Analysis

Workshop Presentations

- PQP Presentation
- Quality Cost Estimate
- Benefit Analysis (Value Added)

EXHIBIT H–1. WORKSHOP 1 (CONT.)

Summary and Questions

■ Background on Quality in IPA
  • Why, What, How
■ Exercise
  • Typical Project Chronology

Critique

■ Handouts
■ Complete Critiques
■ Complete Attendance Roster

Mock Surveillance Exercise

- Example Project Files
- Prepare Checklist

Presentation of Mock Surveillance

- Results (D&CARs)

EXHIBIT H–1. WORKSHOP 1 (CONT.)

Additional OPAS Topics

- Self Assessment/Readiness Review
- Procurement
- Field Change
- Field Surveillance
- D&CAR
- Corrective Action/Followup
- Monthly Report

More OPAS Functions

- Outside Audit Contact Point
- Help Set Up Systems
- Advise PM and Project Staff
- Receipt Inspections

Quality Workshop for Performance Assurance Managers (PAMs)

CH2M HILL

Acronyms Used in This Presentation

- PM Project Manager
- OPAS - Onsite Performance Assurance Specialist
- PAM - Performance Assurance Manager
- D&CAR - Deficiency and Corrective Action Report
- QMP - Quality Management Plan
- SOW - Statement of Work
- PQP - Project Quality Plan
- SSC - Site Safety Coordinator

EXHIBIT H–2. WORKSHOP 2 (CONT.)

Objective and Scope

■ Familiarize You With:
  • Quality Management Program
  • IPA Organization
  • PAM Responsibilities
■ Provide You With Tools to Serve as PAM

Videotaped Message From the President

■ Top Management Support Is Essential
■ Quality Is Everyone's Responsibility
■ Quality Effort Must Add Value
■ Quality Management Will Help Reduce Risk

Concerns and Expectations

- Concerns About Your Role as PAM
- Your Expectations for This Workshop
- Our Expectations for This Workshop

Capsule and Contents

- Why Integrate Quality Into PAM Duties?
- What Is the Basis of Quality Program?
- How Does the PAM Fit in?

Why Integrate Quality Into PAM Duties?

- Reduce Risk
- Add Value (CH2M HILL Examples)
- Meet Contract Requirements
- Meet Recognized Standards
- Improve Quality

What Is the Basis of the Quality Program?

- Risk Management
- Graded Approach

How Will We Implement the Program?

- IPA Organization
- PAM Role
  - PAM Job Description
  - Resources
    - QMP
    - Checklists
    - Staff

PAM Roles and Responsibilities

- Project Quality Planning
- Coordinating OPAS Activities
- Checklists
- Tracking
- Training
- Assessment
- Reporting

EXHIBIT H–2. WORKSHOP 2 (CONT.)

OPAS Roles and Responsibilities

- Field Surveillance
- Assistance to PM
- SSC
- Deficiency Identification/Correction
- Reporting

Navigating the QMP

- Structure
- Parts Most Useful to the PAM

EXHIBIT H–2. WORKSHOP 2 (CONT.)

Example Project Planning Walkthrough

- Develop SOW Activity List
- Develop Project Quality Plan (PQP)
  - Application of Risk-Based, Graded Approach
- Quality Cost Estimate Spreadsheet
- Benefit Analysis (Tangible and Intangible Value Added)

PQP to Quality Cost Estimate Decision Diagram

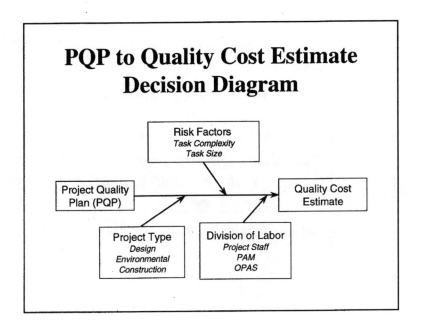

EXHIBIT H–2. WORKSHOP 2 (CONT.)

Explanation of Workshop Assignment

■ Split into Groups
■ Group Presentations
  • Select Activities (Estimate Duration and Cost)
  • Do First Cut of Project Quality Plan and Quality Cost Estimate Spreadsheet
  • Think Graded Approach (Where Are Risks Greatest?)
  • Present Benefit Analysis (Value Added)

Workshop Presentations

■ Scope of Work Summary
■ PQP Matrix and Rationale (Mock Negotiation With Other Groups)
■ Quality Cost Estimate
■ Benefit Analysis (Value Added)

Program Assessment

- Philosophy
- Techniques

Mock Assessment Exercise

- Instructions
- Reporting

Presentation of Mock Assessment Results

Wrapup and Questions

- Background of IPA
  - Why, What, How
- Exercises
  - Project Quality Planning
  - Program Assessment
- Addressed Concerns and Expectations?

Exhibit H–2. Workshop 2 (Cont.)

Critique

- Handouts
- Complete Critiques
- Complete Attendance Roster

EXHIBIT H–3. WORKSHOP 3

PM Quality Workshop

CH2M HILL

Acronyms Used in This Presentation

- PM - Project Manager
- OPAS - Onsite Performance Assurance Specialist
- PAM - Performance Assurance Manager
- D&CAR - Deficiency and Corrective Action Report
- QMP - Quality Management Plan
- SOW - Statement of Work
- PQP - Project Quality Plan
- SSC - Site Safety Coordinator

Objective and Scope

- Familiarize You With:
  - Quality Management Program
  - IPA Organization
  - PAM Responsibities
- Provide You With Tools to Serve as PAM

Videotaped Message From the President

- Top Management Support Is Essential
- Quality Is Everyone's Responsibility
- Quality Effort Must Add Value
- Quality Management Will Help Reduce Risk

Capsule and Contents

- Why IPA?
- What Is Basis of Quality Program?
  How Are We Implementing the Program?
- IPA Organization/Roles
- PAM/OPAS Roles/Responsibilities
- Exercise
  - Project Quality Planning (PQP)

Why Integrated Performance Assurance?

- Similar Support Functions
  - Same Overall Objectives
  - Similar Approaches
- Implements Systems That Make PM Job Easier
- Improves Our Ability to Learn/Improve
- Meet Contract Requirements
- Meet Recognized Standards

EXHIBIT H–3. WORKSHOP 3 (CONT.)

What Is the Basis of the Quality Program?

- Risk Management
  - Ounce of Prevention...
  - Quality Program Implements Project Management Systems That Already Exist
- Graded Approach

How Are We Implementing the Program?

- IPA Organization
- PAM/OPAS Roles and Responsibilities
- Quality Resources
  - QMP
  - Checklists
  - Staff (PAM, OPAS, Quality Director)
- Teamwork

IPA Organization

- Integrated Program Direction
- Services Delivered Through Local Project Staff Trained by IPA
- Services Delivered to:
  - Business Development & PMs-Bid/NoBid Risk Evaluation

IPA Organization *(continued)*

- Project Delivery Managers-Risk Management Plans, (PQP, Health and Safety Plan)
- PMs-H&S, QA, Compliance Consultation, Surveillance, Assessment
- Client Service Managers/Regional Business Group Managers-Project Performance Data

EXHIBIT H–3. WORKSHOP 3 (CONT.)

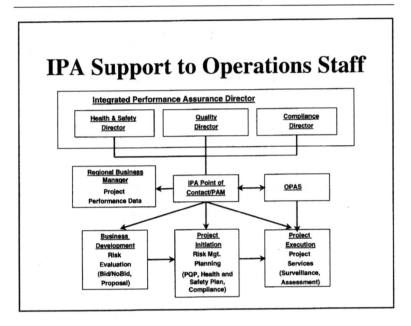

IPA Support to Operations Staff

Integrated Performance Assurance Director

| Health & Safety Director | Quality Director | Compliance Director |

Regional Business Manager
Project Performance Data

IPA Point of Contact/PAM

OPAS

Business Development
Risk Evaluation
(Bid/NoBid, Proposal)

Project Initiation
Risk Mgt. Planning
(PQP, Health and Safety Plan, Compliance)

Project Execution
Project Services
(Surveillance, Assessment)

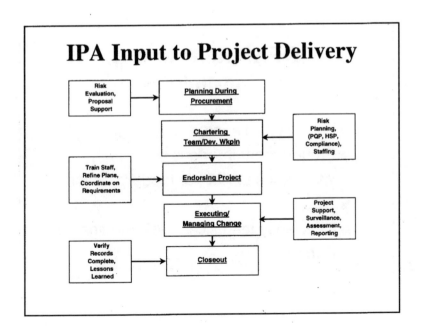

IPA Input to Project Delivery

Risk Evaluation, Proposal Support

Planning During Procurement

Risk Planning, (PQP, HSP, Compliance), Staffing

Chartering Team/Dev. Wkpln

Train Staff, Refine Plans, Coordinate on Requirements

Endorsing Project

Project Support, Surveillance, Assessment, Reporting

Executing/ Managing Change

Verify Records Complete, Lessons Learned

Closeout

PAM Roles and Responsibilities

- PM Interface
- Project Quality Planning (PQP)
- Procurement Interface
- Coordinating OPAS Activities
- Assessment/Audit/Deficiency Reporting (D&CAR)
- Tracking/Trending
- Reporting

OPAS Roles and Responsibilities

- Field Surveillance
- Procurement Interface
- Assistance to PM (Graded Approach)
- SSC
- Deficiency Identification/Correction
- Reporting

Project Chronology

- Business Development
  - IPA Bid-NoBid Risk Evaluation
- Project Delivery
  - IPA Identify and Develop Necessary Plans
- PM
  - Project Support (Consulting, Surveillance, Assessment)

Example Project Planning Walkthrough

- Navigating the QMP
- Develop SOW Activity List
- Develop Project Quality Plan (PQP)
  - Application of Risk Based Graded Approach
- Quality Cost Estimate Spreadsheet
- Benefit Analysis (Tangible and Intangible Value Added)

EXHIBIT H–3. WORKSHOP 3 (CONT.)

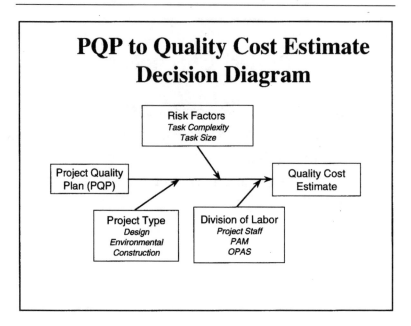

PQP to Quality Cost Estimate Decision Diagram

PQP Preparation Practice

- SOW Summary
- PQP Preparation
- Costing
- Value Added

EXHIBIT H–3. WORKSHOP 3 (CONT.)

Summary and Questions

- Background on Quality in IPA
  - Why, What, How
- Exercise
  - Typical Project Chronology

Discussion and Critique

- Handouts
- Complete Critiques
- Complete Attendance Roster

INTERNET ADDRESSES (URLs) FOR COMPANIES AND ORGANIZATIONS

The Internet provided an easy way to tap into the global trends in IPA by using readily available browsers and search engines. Information about IPA can be found in a variety of Web sites and through electronic correspondence, both archived and real-time. Commercial firms, governmental departments, and standard-setting agencies all publish information on the Web about IPA or related activities. Several standard-setting agencies also serve as electronic bulletin boards and collect correspondence on many IPA and related topics. The following list of Internet addresses (URLs) was current at the time this book was written.

SGE - Sistemi Gestionali Ecocompatibili	http://193.207.147.252/sge/
NCQA HOME PAGE	http://www.ncqa.org/
Software Source: Quality	http://www.softwaresource.com/qual1.htm
KODAK: Health, Safety, and Environment	http://www.kodak.com./aboutKodak/corpInfo/environment/mission.shtml
MKS-Bouw	http://www.tno.nl:8080/instit/bouw/info/products/mks_b.html
Welcome to SR&QA	http://nasarc1.arc.nasa.gov/
BHP Steel - Safety, Health and Environment	http://www.bhp.com.au/steel/health/index.html
MGMT Alliances Inc.	http://www.mgmt14k.com/company.htm
MedNet Quality Improvement Connections	http://www.sermed.com/quality.htm
Integrated Safety Management in Nordic Industry	http://www.vtt.fi/manu/safety/projects/nordic/internet.htm
Lore	http://www.world-net.net:80/home/harrisbc/lackland/metrics_objective1_top_metric.htm
Welcome to ASQC	http://www.asqc.org:80/
SOUTH EAST WATER LIMITED	http://www.sewl.com.au:80/envpol1.html
Re: ISO 9000/ISO 14001 Integration	http://qualitymag.com.:80/wwwboard/messages/
Quality Online, January 1997: the Quality Pro Is Key in Pursuit of ISO 14000	http://bizserve.com:80/qualitymag.com/0197f1.html
Employers' Association ISO and Your Safety & Health Program Seminar	http://www.eaconnect.com:80/iso.html
Quality Progress magazine	http://qualityprogress.asqc.org/
HCI Consulting's Australian Management Topics Articles	http://www.hci.com.au:80/hci/articles/losing.html
Winners Showcase	http://www.quality.nist.gov/show.htm
Welcome to ISO Online	http://www.iso.ch/
ISO 14000 Building Blocks	http://www.rfweston.com/sd/iso.htm
ISO Standards Discussion: Re: INTEGRATION: ISO With Other Initiatives/Felix	http://www.pacemail.com/hyper/iso9000/
ISO Series	http://www.cyberplex.com/bizlink/Content/plant/10-28-96/f16_features.html
Metrics	http://www.prosci.com:80/metrics.htm
DOE Environment, Safety and Health Performance Measures	http://tis-hq.eh.doe.gov:80/web/oeaf/performance_measures/performance_measures.html
Why Integrate ISO Standards?	http://www.isi-standards.org:80/why_iso.htm
FAQ's About ISO 9000	http://www.io.org/~globus/faq.html

Index